KNOPF MAPGUIDES

Welcome to Boston!

This opening fold-out contains a general map of Boston to help you visualize the six large districts discussed in this guide, and four pages of valuable information, handy tips and useful addresses.

Discover Boston through six districts and six maps

A Back Bay / South End
B West End / Beacon Hill / Boston Common
C Chinatown / Financial District / Theater District
D North End / Waterfront
E Fenway / Kenmore / Brookline
F Cambridge

For each district there is a double page of addresses (restaurants – listed in ascending order of price – cafés, bars and stores), followed by a fold-out map for the relevant area with the essential places to see (indicated on the map by a star ★). These places are by no means all that Boston has to offer, but to us they are unmissable. The grid-referencing system (**A** B2) makes it easy for you to pinpoint addresses quickly on the map.

Transportation and hotels in Boston
The last fold-out consists of a transportation map and four pages of practical information that include a selection of hotels.

Thematic index
Lists all the street names, sites and monuments featured in this guide.

COMMONWEALTH AVENUE

world. Halloween (31st).

November

Veteran's Day (11th); Thanksgiving (end Nov).

December

Lighting of the Christmas tree in the Prudential Center, lighting of Boston Common and Public Garden by the mayor.

New Year's Eve: First Night events take over downtown.

OPENING TIMES

Restaurants, bars

Daily 11.30am–10pm (close earlier on Sun); some of the trendier restaurants serve late-night menus. Bars usually close between 1 and 2am. The drinking age is 21.

Stores

Mon-Sat 10am–6/7pm; Sun noon–6pm. Department stores and shopping malls: usually Mon-Sat 10am–8/9pm; Sun noon–6pm.

Museums

Daily 9am–5pm (extended hours on Fri).

Banks, offices

Mon-Fri 8am–4pm; some banks are open Sat am.

EATING OUT

A crop of new, chic restaurants has brought energy to the city's historically conservative dining scene. Traditional restaurants still close by 10pm, but some in trendier areas like the South End transform into lounges around midnight.

Tips

Around 15% is expected (roughly triple the tax amount shown on the bill), 20% for dinner in a nicer restaurant. In bars about $1 per drink.

SHOWS

Reservations

Ticketmaster

→ Tel. (617) 931-2000

www.ticketmaster.com

Reservations and ticket

sales for various venues around the city.

Telecharge

→ www.telecharge.com

Tel. (800) 432-7250

Reduced-price tickets

Bostix

→ www.artsboston.org/ bostix.cfm

Half-price tickets go on sale at 10am (11am Sun) for same-day shows at Faneuil Hall and Copley Square booths. In-person only.

Movie and show listings

→ Boston Globe

www.boston.com

→ Boston Phoenix

www.bostonphoenix.com

Listings for major and minor music, nightlife and art events.

→ Stuff@Night magazine

Bi-weekly with nightlife listings.

NIGHTLIFE

Almost all of Boston's nighttime haunts close at 2am, but that just means

BOSTON ARCHITECTURE

Colonial (17th to early 18th century) Wood frame or clapboard, few remain because of 18th-century fires; **Paul Revere House.**

Federal (1763–1844) Charles Bulfinch is credited with popularizing this style, drawing on Greek Revival; **New State House, Harrison Gray Otis House.**

Victorian (19th century) Borrowed from Italian Renaissance, neo-Gothic and neo-Romanesque; **Boston Public Library, Trinity Church.**

Contemporary

I. M. Pei's John Hancock Tower is the most famous skyscraper, but new projects are pushing the city's architectural boundaries: the **Ray and Maria Strata Center** and the new **Institute of Contemporary Art.**

BOSTON VIEWS

From the Prudential Skywalk Observatory (see **A**) Splurge for a drink two floors up, at the Top o the Hub restaurant.

From the Bunker Hill Monument (see **D**) Climb the 294 steps to the top of the Bunker Hill Monument for a bird's-eye view of the city and harbor.

From the water The last part of a Duck Tour (see box above right) is spent on the River Charles.

From the T Despite the unglamorous setting, one of the most satisfying views of Boston and Cambridge appears as you're riding the Red Line between the Charles/MGH and Kendall/MIT T stops.

PUBLIC GARDEN LAKE

NEW AND OLD MEET IN DOWNTOWN

CITY PROFILE

■ Capital of Massachusetts, nicknamed the 'Cradle of Liberty' for its important role in the American Revolution ■ 600,000 inhabitants ■ 48.4 square miles ■ More than 12 million visitors a year

REVOLUTIONARY DATES

1620 Pilgrims begin the first New England settlement at Plymouth Harbor **1629** John Winthrop and the Massachusetts Bay Colony establish Boston **March 5, 1770** The death of five Bostonians at the hands of British soldiers is known as the Boston Massacre **Dec 16, 1773** Boston Tea Party: rebels protest taxation by dumping 342 crates of tea into the harbor **1775** Battles of Lexington and Concord mark the beginning of the Revolutionary War **July 4, 1776** Declaration of Independence is ratified in Philadelphia and declared in Boston.

BOSTON ON THE NET

→ *www.bostonusa.com*
Boston Convention and Visitors Bureau website.
→ *www.cityofboston.gov*
Information for residents and visitors.
→ *www.boston.com*
Online home of the *Boston Globe*.
→ *www.boston.citysearch.com*
Listings and reviews for restaurants, bars, shops and venues.

TOURIST INFO

Greater Boston Convention and Visitors Bureau (A C-D3)
→ *2 Copley Place, Suite 105*
Tel. (888) 733-2678
www.bostonusa.com
Open 24 hours
CVS Drugstore **(A** D2)
→ *587 Boylston St*
Tel. (617) 437-8414
Store 24 **(A** C2)
→ *717 Boylston St*
Tel. (617) 424-6888

British Consulate General (east of **F** F4)
→ *One Memorial Drive, Suite 1500, Cambridge, MA 02142*
Tel. (617) 245-4500
www.britainusa.com/boston

TELEPHONE

The area code for Boston is 617. Its immediate suburbs use area code 857.
To call Boston from Europe
Dial 00 + 1 (US) + area code + the 7-digit number.
To call abroad from Boston
Dial 011 + country code + area code and number.
Directory enquiries
Tel. 411 (national)
Tel. 00 (international)
Numbers beginning with 1-800 and 888 are free of charge.
Emergencies
Police, fire brigade
Tel. 911

PUBLIC HOLIDAYS

New Year's Day; Martin Luther King Jr Day (3rd Mon in Jan); **Presidents' Day** (3rd Mon in Feb); **Patriot's Day** (3rd Mon in April); **Memorial Day** (last Mon in May); July 4; **Labor Day** (1st Mon in Sep); **Columbus Day** (2nd Mon in Oct); **Veterans Day** (Nov 11); **Thanksgiving** (3rd Thu in Nov); **Christmas Day.**

DIARY OF EVENTS

January/early February
Martin Luther King Jr Day (3rd Mon). Chinese New Year with fireworks and parade (Chinatown).
March
St Patrick's Day (17th): rowdy parade in South Boston and celebrations across the city.
April
Patriot's Day (3rd Mon): Boston Marathon from Hopkington to Copley

Square. Major League Baseball season begins.
May
Memorial Day (last Mon). Lilac Sunday (3rd Sun): Arnold Arboretum is awash in violet and visitors are allowed to picnic.
June/July
Annual Harborfest (late June-July 4): concerts and the ever-popular Chowderfest. Fourth of July free Boston Pops at the Hatch Shell followed by spectacular fireworks over the Charles.
August
The last month of free Friday night movies at the Hatch Shell; Chinatown Festival (early Aug).
September
Gorgeous fall foliage signals the beginning of 'leaf-peeping' season.
October
Columbus Day (2nd Mon); Head of the Charles Regatta (3rd weekend): largest rowing race in the

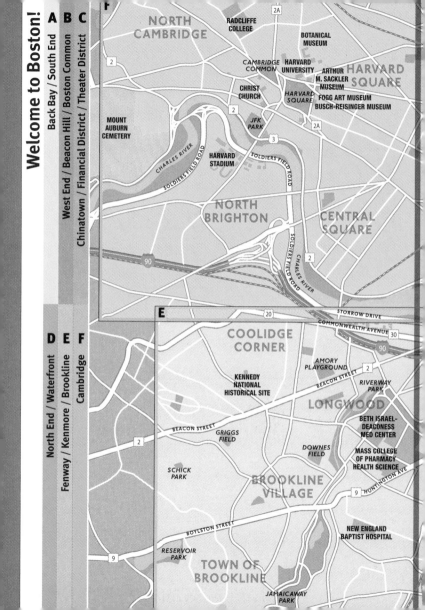

Welcome to Boston!

A Back Bay / South End

B West End / Beacon Hill / Boston Common

C Chinatown / Financial District / Theater District

D North End / Waterfront

E Fenway / Kenmore / Brookline

F Cambridge

NORTH CAMBRIDGE

RADCLIFFE COLLEGE

BOTANICAL MUSEUM

CAMBRIDGE COMMON

HARVARD UNIVERSITY

ARTHUR M. SACKLER MUSEUM

HARVARD SQUARE

CHRIST CHURCH

HARVARD SQUARE

FOGG ART MUSEUM

BUSCH-REISINGER MUSEUM

MOUNT AUBURN CEMETERY

JFK PARK

CHARLES RIVER

HARVARD STADIUM

SOLDIERS FIELD ROAD

SOLDIERS FIELD ROAD

NORTH BRIGHTON

CENTRAL SQUARE

SOLDIERS FIELD ROAD

CHARLES RIVER

90

STORROW DRIVE

COMMONWEALTH AVENUE

COOLIDGE CORNER

AMORY PLAYGROUND

KENNEDY NATIONAL HISTORICAL SITE

BEACON STREET

RIVERWAY PARK

LONGWOOD

BETH ISRAEL-DEACONESS MED CENTER

BEACON STREET

GRIGGS FIELD

DOWNES FIELD

MASS COLLEGE OF PHARMACY HEALTH SCIENCE

SCHICK PARK

BROOKLINE VILLAGE

HUNTINGTON AVE

9

BOYLSTON STREET

NEW ENGLAND BAPTIST HOSPITAL

RESERVOIR PARK

TOWN OF BROOKLINE

9

JAMAICAWAY PARK

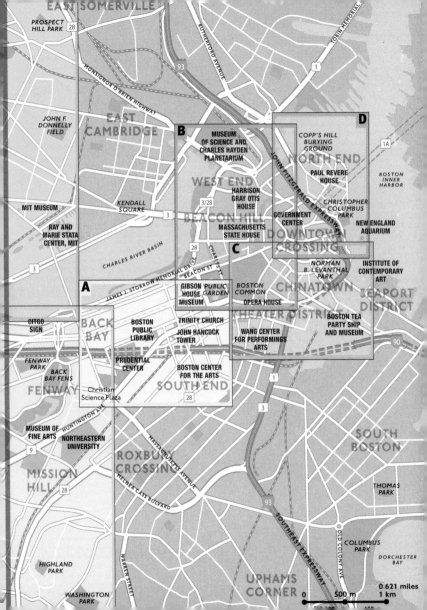

QUINCY MARKET

THE BOSTON SKYLINE

DOWNTOWN CROSSING

A READING ROOM IN ONE OF HARVARD UNIVERSITY'S BUILDINGS

Boston's best department stores

Barneys New York (A C3)
→ *100 Huntington Ave (Copley Place)*
Tel. (617) 385-3300 Mon-Sat 10am-9pm; Sun 11am-6pm
This 45,000-sq-ft space has the same cheeky displays and boutique vibe as the New York flagship. There's a 4,000-sq-ft shoe salon, complete with working fireplace.

Filene's Basement (C C2)
→ *234 Washington St*
Tel. (617) 348-7974
Mon-Sat 9.30am (9am Sat)–8pm; Sun 11am-7pm
Bins overflow with designer denim, while the high-end Vault carries cut-rate Prada, Versace and D&G. Items get cheaper the longer they stay in the store.

Louis Boston (A E2)
→ *234 Berkeley St*
Tel. (800) 225-5135
Mon 11am-6pm; Tue-Sat 10am-7pm (6pm Tue-Wed)
A house of style with salon,

apothecary and mini music store, this is still the best place to find of-the-moment designers like Marni, Project Alabama and Zac Posen.

Downtown Crossing (C B2)
→ *Tel. (617) 482-2139*
www.downtowncrossing.org
A pedestrian mall with mostly chain stores such as H&M and Designer Shoe Warehouse.

Neiman Marcus (A C-D3)
→ *5 Copley Place*
Tel. (617) 536-3660 Mon-Sat 10am-8pm; Sun noon-6pm
The only New England branch is an elegant three-story store in tony Copley Place. AmEx-bearing Bostonians (it's the only card accepted) come for designers like Derek Lam, Chloe, and Missoni, as well as a huge selection of haute denim and cosmetics.

Specialty shopping: vintage clothes

Oonas (F B2)

→ *1210 Massachusetts Ave*
Tel. (617) 491-2654
Mon-Sat 11am-7pm (8pm Fri); Sun noon-6pm
A funky thrift shop with Stepford wife house-dresses, retro band T-shirts and faux fur jackets.

Garment District (F F3)
→ *200 Broadway*
Tel. (617) 876-5230
www.garment-district.com
A vast collection of vintage and thrifts, including the cult favorite Dollar-a-Pound area.

For gourmets

Formaggio Kitchen (A F4)
→ *268 Shawmut Ave*
Tel. (617) 350-6996
Mon-Sat 9am-8pm (7pm Sat); Sun 11am-5pm
An epicurean paradise with everything but organic San Benedetto jams to artisanal Jasper Hill cheeses. Delicious selection of sandwiches and salads to take out. Another outlet is at 244 Huron Ave, Cambridge (**F** A-B1).

BOSTON ON FOOT

Boston is known as America's Walking City and with good reason – almost all the major historical and cultural sites are clustered together. The National Park Service provides the following trails:

The Freedom Trail
A very popular 2.5-mile redbrick trail that begins at Boston Common and highlights the major historical sights of Beacon Hill, the North End, and Charlestown. Guided tours and maps available at the following address:
Boston National Historical Park Visitor Center
→ *15 State St*
Tel. (617) 242-5642
www.thefreedomtrail.org

Black Heritage Trail
It covers 1.6 miles of Beacon Hill and downtown, and includes the Robert Gould Shaw memorial and the African Meeting House. Guided tours available.
→ *46 Joy St*
Tel. (617) 725-0022
Mon-Sat 10am-4pm.
www.afroammuseum.org

Boston Women's Heritage Trail
A guidebook of nine walking tours that emphasize women's contributions to different Boston neighborhoods. Available from:
The Boston Common Visitors Information Booth
→ *147 Tremont St*
Tel. (617) 426-3115
Mon-Sat 8.30am-5pm; Sun 10am-6pm

ARBORFEST

BOSTON DUCK TOURS

ANEUIL HALL

A WALK ON THE CAMBRIDGE SIDE

TOURS

Boston Harbor Cruises
→ 1 Long Wharf
Tel. (617) 542-8000; www.bostonharborcruises.com
Water tours, including whale watches aboard high-speed catamarans and sunset cruises. Groups can charter one of the company's 23 boats for a party or day trip.

Boston Duck Tours
→ Tel. (617) 723-3825
www.bostonducktours.com
The original and still the best: the brightly hued WWII-era amphibious craft may look silly, but the guides are hilarious and the views from the Charles River unbeatable.

that the party starts a little earlier.

Dance clubs
The club scene is centered around Lansdowne St near Fenway and Tremont St in the Theater District. Check the *Stuff@Night* and *Phoenix* listings.

Live music
Between MIT and Harvard Square, Massachusetts Ave has a handful of funky live music venues. Beyond that, there are pockets of counter-mainstream-culture throughout the city. National acts such as Mariah Carey and the Red Hot Chili Peppers pack the TD Banknorth Garden (formerly the Fleet Center). Classical music fans will have to go to the Theater District or Symphony Hall.

Club Passim (**E** F3)
→ 47 Palmer St
Tel. (617) 492-7679
Daily 11am–11pm
Hidden underground off a small alleyway, this earthy

acoustic music venue is a leftover from Harvard's early days. Small tables filled with aging hippies and bookish locals, and unknown or national folk artists on stage. Tickets around $15.

The Burren (north of **D** A1)
→ 247 Elm St
Tel. (617) 776-6896
Daily 10am–1am
Live Irish music nightly and surprisingly good bands. Cover charge on weekends.

The Middle East (**E** F2)
→ 472 Massachusetts Ave
Tel. (617) 492-9181
www.mideastclub.com
This Central Square institution has three performance stages, two bars and three restaurants. Live shows nightly, from up-and-coming local bands to belly dancing. Tickets from $10–$20.

Cantab Lounge (**E** F2)
→739 Massachusetts Ave
Tel (617) 354-2685
Mon-Sat 8am–1am (2am Thu-Sat); Sun noon–1am

This lovably downtrodden live music venue features everything from comedy to spoken word. On Wed nights, 'Little' Joe Cook performs an upbeat blues and R&B lineup for a loyal, eclectic crowd. Cover charge varies.

MARKETS

Antiques and crafts
Cambridge Antique Market (**B** B2)
→ 201 Msgr O'Brien Hwy
Tel. (617) 868-9655
www.marketantique.com
Five floors and 150 dealers, with a wide range of items and quality.

Cambridge Artists Cooperative (**A** F2)
→ 59A Church St
Tel. (617) 868-4434
A three-story shop packed with art, crafts and clothes by local artisans.

Farmers' markets
www.massfarmersmarkets.org
Copley Square (**A** D2)
→ St James Ave, in front of

Trinity Church.
May-Nov: Tue, Fri 11am–6pm
City Hall (**B** D4)
→ City Hall Plaza.
May-Nov: Mon, Wed 11am–6pm
Haymarket (**D** A5)
→ Blackstone St
Fri-Sat during daylight hours

SHOPPING

Where to shop
Boston's shopping scene is more hip and extensive than it gets credit for. On Newbury St there are hot young designers and one-of-a-kind jewelry. In the South End, new galleries and boutiques spring up daily, and Charles St is packed with antiques dealers and preppy enclaves. In the less-traveled streets of greater Cambridge, there are funky thrift stores and ethnic import shops. Downtown Crossing is still the best place to get a bargain.

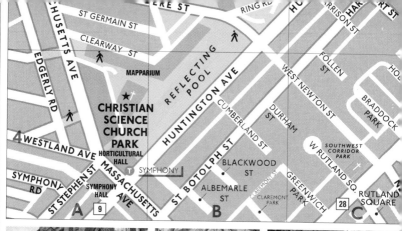

BOSTON CENTER FOR THE ARTS Ω

PRUDENTIAL SHOPS

MAPPARIUM

Newbury Street (A A-E2)
→ www.newbury-st.com
This 'Rodeo Drive of the East' is a two-mile-long tree-lined strip of shops and cafés. Made up of elegant low brownstones, it caters as much to people watching as it does to designer shopping sprees, especially in the spring, when restaurants open their patios.

John Hancock Tower (A D2)
→ 200 Clarendon St
I. M. Pei's 62-story sleek mirrored glass skyscraper dominates Boston's relatively low skyline and is a useful visual landmark when wandering around the city. The observatory on the 60th floor has not reopened since September 11.

Boston Public Library (A C2)
→ 700 Boylston St
Tel. (617) 536-5400
Mon-Sat 9am–9pm (5pm Fri-Sat); Sun 1–5pm in Oct-May
America's oldest library has a stately façade and an elevated entrance flanked by statues symbolizing Art and Science. There are two wings: the original research library designed as a Renaissance palazzo by McKim, Mead and White, and the 1972 Philip Johnson addition, the General Library. The McKim has John Adams' personal library,

John Singer Sargent murals, and a peaceful outdoor courtyard.

Trinity Church (A D2)
→ 206 Clarendon St
Tel. (617) 536-0944
Tue-Sun 9am–6pm; services Sun, Tue, Wed and Thu
One of the city's architectural treasures, it was designed in the late 1800s by Henry Hobson Richardson and exemplifies his Romanesque style. The neutral granite and sandstone exterior gives way to a vibrant interior dominated by stained glass windows, including a number of layered opalescent works by John LeFarge.

Copley Square (A D2)
→ Farmers' market May – Nov 21: Tue, Fri 11am–6p
Bookended by Trinity Church and the Boston Public Library, this tree shaded plaza serves as the hub of the Back Ba area. The Boston Mara finishes here every yea and during the warmer months there are musi festivals and regular farmers' markets with organic produce, cut flowers, and baked goo

Gibson House Museum (A D1)
→ 137 Beacon St
Tel. (617) 267-6338
Guided tours 1pm, 2pm and 3pm

A

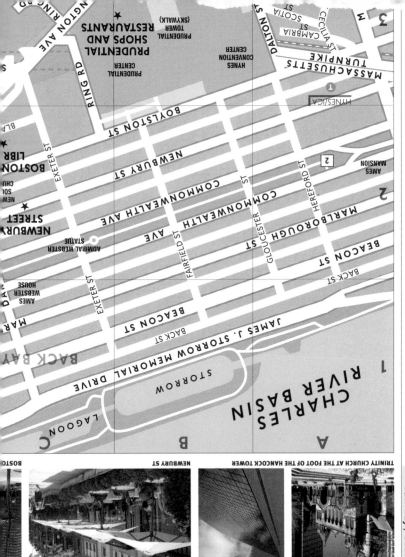

TRINITY CHURCH AT THE FOOT OF THE HANCOCK TOWER

NEWBURY ST

BOSTO

An unsightly pond until the mid-19th century, Back Bay is a neighborhood of patrician brownstones set on landfill. Newbury Street is Boston's chicest thoroughfare, studded with upscale retailers and stylish cafés. Just beyond, scenic Copley Square is surrounded by instantly recognizable cultural and architectural landmarks. Five minutes away, the up-and-here neighborhood of the South End continues to grow, both in size – now encompassing the gallery-filled SoWa, or South of Washington St area – and in reputation. This is Boston's best claim to hipness, with Manhattan-grade chefs, avant-garde galleries and sky-high real estate values.

Throughout this book, the à la carte prices refer to a two-course meal, excluding drinks or service.

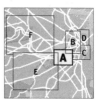

SONSIE

VIA MATTA

RESTAURANTS

Steve's Greek Restaurant (A A2)
→ 316 Newbury St
Tel. (617) 267-1817
Mon-Sat 7.30am–11pm;
Sun 10am–10pm
Despite its prime location this low-key restaurant serves unpretentious, inexpensive food in generous portions.
À la carte $15.

Via Matta (A F2)
→ 79 Park Plaza
Tel. (617) 422-0008 Mon-Fri
11.30am–2.30pm, 5.30–
10pm (11pm Fri); Sat 5–11pm
Less pricey than its sister eatery Radius (see **C**) – also owned by executive chef Michael Schlow and Christopher Myers – this Italian restaurant prepares perfect, simple dishes with the best ingredients. Don't miss the Mascaporeos, crisp chocolate shortbread with sweet mascarpone cream.
À la carte $35.

Aquitaine (A E4)
→ 569 Tremont St
Tel. (617) 424-8577
Daily 5.30–10pm (11pm Thu-Sat); Sat-Sun 10am–3pm
Popular and delicious bistro fare and a casual atmosphere. Great brunch menu – try the brioche French toast with

caramelized pear compote Award-winning wine list.
À la carte $35.

B&G Oysters (A E4)
→ 550 Tremont St
Tel. (617) 423-0550
Mon-Fri 11.30am–11pm (10pr Mon); Sat-Sun noon–11pm (10pm Sun)
Chef-owner Barbara Lynch's stylish South End restaurant is the original gourmet clam shack. The B.L.T. with lobster has a loyal following, but purists go for the lobster roll, served with very crisp fries Raw bar serving 12 varietie of oysters. À la carte $40.

Grill 23 (A E2)
→ 161 Berkeley St
Tel. (617) 542-2255
Daily 5.30–10.30pm
(11pm Fri-Sat; 10pm Sun)
This restaurant, with its brass lamps and mahogan paneling, is celebrated for its dry-aged steaks and shamelessly indulgent menu (truffled 'tater tots' and kobe beef steak tartare). Over 1,500 wines.
À la carte $60.

Hamersley's Bistro (A E4
→ 553 Tremont St
Tel. (617) 423-2700
Daily 6–10pm (10.30pm Sat; 9.30pm Sun)
Despite the influx of newer flashier restaurants, this remains the South End's favorite. Chef-owner Gordo

AR

DYPTIQUE

MARC JACOBS

Hamersley and his wife, Fiona, serve refined French bistro fare in a warm, homey environment. Dishes reflect the best of the seasons, but the perfect roast chicken with garlic, lemon and parsley is a perennial favorite. À la carte $50.

BARS, CAFÉS

Armani Café (**A** C2)
→ 214 Newbury St
Tel. (617) 437-0909 Daily 11.30am–11pm (1am Thu-Sat)
Pouty-lipped waitstaff turn this chic, open, spartan space into a catwalk. The light Italian fare is surprisingly good, and in warm weather, try to get a table outdoors. $20.

Oak Bar, Fairmont Copley Plaza (**A** D2)
→ 138 St. James Ave
Tel. (617) 267-5300 Daily 11am–midnight (1am Fri-Sat)
In this sumptuous lounge, richly appointed with dark wood, pearly marble and gleaming gilt, well-turned-out men and women sip carefully mixed cocktails from an extensive martini menu. Live music Tue-Sat.

Parish Café (**A** E2)
→ 361 Boylston St
Tel. (617) 247-4777 Daily 11.30am (noon Sun)–2am
A cozy spot with a star-studded menu: the sandwiches are all created by celebrated chefs. Ana Sortun does an amazing fried mussels-stuffed baguette. Nice outdoor patio. $10.

Sonsie (**A** A2)
→ 327 Newbury St
Tel. (617) 351-2500
Daily 11.30am–1am
This trendy café is popular for mid-spree refueling. At night, the young and glamorous head downstairs to the posh Red Room Lounge. Chic setting and view.

SHOPPING

Newbury Street (**A** A-E2)
Anchored by Burberry and Chanel, this street has impressive designer boutiques, art galleries and beauty bars.

Barbara Krakow Gallery, at no. 10
→ Tel. (617) 262-4490
Tue-Sat 10am–5.30pm
Mostly modern art, with big names such as Richard Serra and Roy Lichtenstein, as well as rising stars.

Queen Bee, at no. 85
→ Tel. (617) 859-7999
Mon-Sat 10am–6pm (7pm Fri-Sat); Sun noon–6pm
Preppy clothes and Milly, CK Bradley and Diane von Furstenberg.

Marc Jacobs, at no. 91
→ Tel. (617) 425-0404
Both the gently priced Marc items and men's and women's collections.

Diptyque, at no. 123
→ Tel. (617) 351-2430
Mon-Sat 10am–6pm; Sun noon–6pm
Perfumes, candles, soaps and bath oils are in this flagship store of the legendary Paris fragrance house.

Second Time Around, at no. 176
→ Tel. (617) 247-3504
Mon-Sat 11am–7pm (10am Sat); Sun noon–6pm
You can unearth amazing finds at this chic consignment shop – Manolo, Oscar, Miuccia, at 25–50% original retail.

Whim, at no. 253
→ Tel. (617) 437-7600
Mon-Sat 11am–7pm; Sun noon–6pm
A mix of carefully chosen designers, including Barbara Bui and Sigerson Morrison, as well unique vintage jewelry.

Jasmine Sola, at no. 344
→ Tel. (617) 867-4636
Mon-Sat 10am–8pm (9pm Fri-Sat); Sun noon–7pm
High-end contemporary clothing, always packed with students clamoring for James Perse tops or Rock & Republic jeans.

Three other outlets in Cambridge.

South of Washington St Galleries (SoWa) (**A** F4)
→ 450 Harrison Ave
This former mill has five galleries and more than 20 artists' studios. Some of the most popular include:

Bromfield Gallery (#27)
Tel. (617) 451-3605
Wed-Sat noon–5pm
A cooperative run by 20 artists with a wide range of styles and mediums – from abstract painting to conceptual sculpture.

Genovese/Sullivan Gallery
Enter at 47 Thayer St
Tel. (617) 426-9738
Tue-Sat 10.30am–5.30pm
Young contemporary artists from around the country.

Boston Sculptors Gallery
Enter at 486 Harrison Ave
Tel. (617) 482-7781
Tue-Sat 11am–6pm
A 28-artist cooperative featuring two different sculptors each month.

Shreve, Crump & Low (**A** E2)
→ 440 Boylston St
Tel. (617) 267-9100 Mon-Sat 10am–6pm (7pm Thu)
The city's most esteemed jeweler has everything from cufflinks to baby rattles. Don't miss designs from Vera Wang and Kieselstein-Cord.

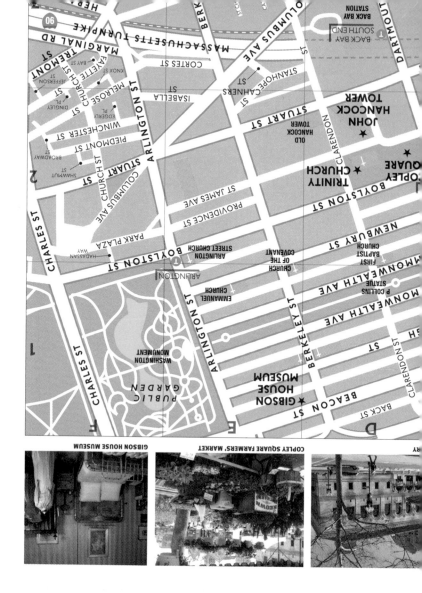

GIBSON HOUSE MUSEUM

COPLEY SQUARE FARMERS' MARKET

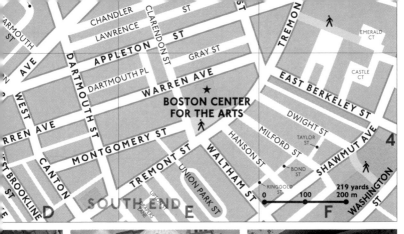

CHRISTIAN SCIENCE CHURCH AND POOL

MARY BAKER EDDY LIBRARY

ssic 1859 brownstone e outside, inside this eum is a time warp of rian-era Back Bay, erved almost exactly in riginal state, including wallpaper, bedroom and dressing gowns. of the house's six es are open to visitors, ding the servants' ters and the Gibson y bedrooms.

on Center he Arts (A E4)

9 Tremont St, between ley and Clarendon 17) 426-5000 four-acre compound des the Cyclorama da, a performing arts xhibition venue; the

Tremont Estates building, with over 50 artist workspaces; and the Mills Gallery, the site of BCA's six major annual exhibits. Recently, the über-hip Atelier 505 mixed-use complex, with luxury condos, restaurants and shops, has attracted even more energy to the area.

Prudential shops and restaurants (A B-C3)

The base of this 52-story skyscraper is occupied by the Prudential Center, a collection of shops and restaurants, including Lacoste, Crane & Co., Sephora and California Pizza Kitchen. Gucci, Dior, Tiffany are across the

elevated bridge to Copley Place. Don't miss the views from the Prudential Center Skywalk on the 50th floor and the Top of the Hub restaurant, two floors up.

Christian Science Church Park (A A4)

The First Church of Christ, Scientist

→ 175 Huntington Ave Tel. (617) 450-2000 Services Sun 10am and 7pm This sprawling 14-acre Plaza is the Christian Science headquarters. The original Romanesque church still stands, alongside the 1960 3,000-person domed extension. In the 1970s a massive fountain that gushes water

40 feet into the air and a vast 98-by-686-foot reflecting pool – a serene oasis in busy Back Bay – were added.

Mary Baker Eddy Library for the Betterment of Humanity

→ 200 Massachusetts Ave Tel. (617) 450-7000 Tue-Sun 10am–4pm A grand 11-story neoclassical building with an exhaustive collection of Christian Science artifacts as well as a few crowd-pleasing exhibits. Inside the Mapparium, a three-story stained-glass globe, you can see the world from the inside out, sans geographical distortion.

STATE HOUSE

MUSEUM OF SCIENCE

Louisburg Square (B B4-5)
→ *Between Pinckney and Mount Vernon sts*
Boston's only remaining private garden square is an enclave of blueblood elitism in the already tony Beacon Hill, with some of the city's most expensive real estate and a stringent home-owners association. Louisa May Alcott once lived here, but the most famous current residents are John Kerry and Teresa Heinz-Kerry.

Boston Common (B C5-6)
This 48-acre green has always been a gathering place – during the early 1800s, it was an arena for both public hangings and communal cattle grazing.

Nowadays, it hosts everything from ice skating in the winter to outdoor performances in summer. Visit the Augustus St Gauden sculpture that pays tribute to Colonel Robert Gould Shaw and his all-black 54th Regiment. Shaw and 270 of his men died in an attack on Fort Ledger during the Civil War.

Public Garden (B B6)
Across from Boston Common, the country's first public botanical garden feels like a bit of Paris. Weeping willows hover delicately over gently curving walking paths, and a miniature suspension bridge cuts across the small

lagoon. In warm weather, take a short ride in pedal-powered swan boats.

State House (B C4)
→ *Beacon and Park sts*
Tel. (617) 727-3676
Mon-Fri 10am–4pm
Echoing his work on the U.S. Capitol, Charles Bulfinch imbued the 1798 Massachusetts seat of government with grandiose sanctity. The striking 30-foot-high dome was initially covered in copper by Paul Revere & Sons in order to prevent leaking, but the glimmering landmark soon became a source of state pride. In 1874 it received a gleaming upgrade: a full sheath of 23.5-karat gold.

You can tour the Hall of Flags, as well as the Ho and Senate chambers.

Charles Street (B B4-
With cobblestone sidew and historically preserv brownstones, this char street is quintessential Boston. Residents of ne Beacon Hill come here the upmarket boutique and well-edited antique shops, as well as the gourmet food shops ar restaurants. The gentle pace and unique stores make for some of the city's best strolling.

Esplanade and Hatch Shell (B A4-5)
Set along the Charles R between the Longfellow

CHARLES STREET

LOUISBURG SQUARE

REVERE ST

LEWIS
HAYDEN
HOUSE

PHILLIPS ST

LINDALL
CRT

BEAC

NORTH
ANDERSON
ST

NORTH
GROVE ST

PARKMAN
ST

CAMBRIDGE
ST AVE

CHARLES/MGH

CAMBRIDGE ST

IGAR HIGH

KMENT RD

REVERE
ST

LONGFELLOW
BRIDGE

MASSACHUSETTS
GENERAL HOSPITAL

BLOSSOM ST

CHARLES ST

CHARLESBANK
PARK

CHARLES RIVER BASIN

WES

SCIENCE PARK

LEVERET
CIRCLE

SCIENCE
PARK

HAYDEN
PLANETARIUM

MUGAR OMNI
THEATER

MUSEUM
OF SCIENCE

CHARLES RIVER DAM

MSGR O'BRIEN HWY

CAMBRIDGE PARKWAY

COMMERCIAL AVE

LECHMERE
CANAL PARK

CAMBRIDGESIDE
GALLERIA

INDUSTRIAL PARK ROAD

CHARLESTOWN AVE

EAST ST

B

A

1

2

3

4

B

Only a half-mile square, Beacon Hill has historically been associated with a certain aristocratic class that Oliver Wendell Holmes famously coined 'Boston Brahmins'. It is still the city's most sought-after neighborhood. Stringent architectural codes have kept it looking much like it did during the 19th century, with stately brick row houses and working gas lampposts. Idyllic Charles Street, with cobblestone sidewalks and upscale boutiques, leads directly to Boston Common and the Public Garden. Bounding these famous green spaces are notable historical sights, including the State House (designed by Charles Bulfinch), and luxury hotels.

PARAMOUNT CAFÉ

BRISTOL LOUNGE

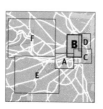

RESTAURANTS

Upper Crust (B B5)
→ 20 Charles St
Tel. (617) 723-9600
Daily 11.30am–10pm
(10.30pm Thu-Sun)
Dominated by a long communal table, the original branch of this gourmet pizza chain has a friendly, good-natured vibe. Chefs stretch dough into impossibly thin pies in the open kitchen. Pizzas around $15.

Figs (B B5)
→ 42 Charles St
Tel. (617) 742-3447
Mon-Fri 5.30–10pm; Sat-Sun noon–10pm (9pm Sun)
One of prolific owner-chef Todd English's grown-up pizzerias. The addictive pies are large, with a tremendous thin crust and creative toppings. Don't miss the fig, prosciutto and gorgonzola pizza. No dessert. À la carte $20.

Lala Rokh (B A5)
→ 90 Mount Vernon St
Tel. (617) 720-5511
Mon-Fri noon–3pm, 5.30–10pm; Sat-Sun 5.30–10pm
Tucked away below street level in a quiet residential area is the city's best Persian cuisine. Azita-Bina Seibel and Babak Bina serve food that they grew up with – rich stews and marinated meats infused with fragrant herbs and spices; the basmati rice is smothered with cumin, cinnamon and rose petals. Perfect for a cozy dinner. À la carte $25.

Torch (B B5)
→ 26 Charles St
Tel. (617) 723-5939
Tue-Sun 5.30–10pm
Classic dishes with French, Italian and Asian accents are offered in this small restaurant with burnished copper walls and floor-to-ceiling windows. Favorites include monkfish on white bean ragout with balsamic brown butter, and a bistro steak with potato gratin and truffle vinaigrette. Don't miss the chocolate mousse and crème brûlée. À la carte $35.

No. 9 Park (B C5)
→ 9 Park St
Tel. (617) 742-9991
Mon-Fri 11.30am–2.30pm, 5.30–10pm; Sat 5.30–10pm
The crown jewel of chef-owner Barbara Lynch's successful restaurant triumvirate. Diners return for Lynch's signature prune-stuffed gnocchi with seared foie gras. The rest of the French- and Italian-influenced menu is equally memorable – for a full immersion, try the nine-course tasting menu.

SIOR   **FLAT OF THE HILL**   **KOO DE KIR**

Reservations essential. À la carte $60.

Excelsior (B B6)
→ 272 Boylston St
Tel. (617) 426-7878
Daily 4.30pm–midnight (2am Fri-Sat)
Adam Tihany designed to impress: you enter via a glass elevator that whisks you up through a vertical 7,000-bottle wine cellar. From there, chef Eric Brennan takes over, justifying the hype with dishes like pork ribeye with an ancho chile-honey glaze, accompanied by asparagus slaw. If it's not a special occasion, stick to the first-floor lounge – you can get elaborate bar food and Brennan's celebrated lobster pizza without breaking the bank. À la carte $60.

BARS, CAFÉS

Paramount Café (B B5)
→ 44 Charles St
Tel. (617) 720-1152
Daily 7am (8am Sat-Sun)–4.30pm, 5–10pm
Beacon Hill's most popular café since 1937. More polished than your typical corner diner, but with the same friendly service and reliably good food. Buttermilk pancakes are popular for brunch,

and the New York sirloin salad with blue cheese is hearty enough for dinner. À la carte $15.

Panificio (B B4)
→ 144 Charles St
Tel. (617) 227-4340
Daily 8am (9.30am Sat-Sun)–9.30pm
Savory focaccias and sugar-dusted pastries tempt passersby to this cozy bakery and café. This is the perfect place for an inexpensive, leisurely breakfast.

The Bristol, The Four Seasons Hotel (B B6)
→ 200 Boylston St
Tel. (617) 351-2053
Sun-Fri 6.30am–11.30pm (12.30am Fri); Sat 7am–12.30am. Afternoon tea daily 3–4.30pm
Business deals are made over power breakfasts and lunches, but it is the lounge's highly civilized afternoon tea that is the real attraction. Ask for a table near the windows so you can look out onto the Public Garden while nibbling at flaky scones with clotted cream and perfect tea sandwiches. Afternoon tea $24.

SHOPPING

Wish (B B5)
→ 49 Charles St

Tel. (617) 227-4441 Mon-Sat 10am–7pm (8pm Thu; 6pm Sat); Sun noon–6pm
A cheerful shop stocked with streamlined Theory separates, embellished Nanette Lepore blazers, and flirty Milly sundresses. Twenty-somethings sick of Newbury Street come here for their preppy chic necessities.

Flat of the Hill (B B4)
→ 60 Charles St
Tel. (617) 619-9977
Tue-Fri 11am–6pm; Sat 10am–5pm; Sun noon–5pm
Everything is very feminine and fun here, from grosgrain belts with rhinestone buckles to embossed picture albums. A perfect place for gifts, with cheeky stationery, candles and covetable Lauren Merkin clutches and Botkier bags.

Koo de Kir (B B4)
→ 65 Charles St
Tel. (617) 723-8111 Mon-Fri 11am–7pm; Sat 10am–5pm; Sun noon–5pm
The name comes from coup de coeur – 'strike to the heart' – and you're bound to be smitten by this design store's original modern goods. An eclectic collection, from a set of nesting bowls resembling a gorgeous head of lettuce to mirrored side tables.

20th Century Limited (B B4)
→ 73 Charles St
Tel. (617) 742-1031 Mon-Sat 11am–6pm; Sun noon–5pm
Everyone is a diva in this vintage jewelry shop, which boasts its own in-house tiara designer. Pick up 1950s Bakelite bangles, costume brooches, or pillbox hats inspired by Jackie O.

Savenor's Market (B B4)
→ 160 Charles St
Tel. (617) 723-6328
Mon-Sat 9am–8.30pm (8pm Sat); Sun noon–7pm
Julia Child used to get all her meat from the Cambridge branch of this fantastic gourmet shop, and celebrated local chefs like Barbara Lynch still shop here. In addition to unusual game offerings such as alligator and camel, there are foodie staples like paté, truffle oil, and imported pasta.

Gallagher-Christopher Antiques (B A5)
→ 84 Chestnut St
Tel. (617) 523-1992
Mon-Sat 11am–6pm
Just the place to find splendid chandeliers and mirrors for a Beacon Hill brownstone. A wide array of English and Continental furniture from the 18th, 19th and 20th centuries.

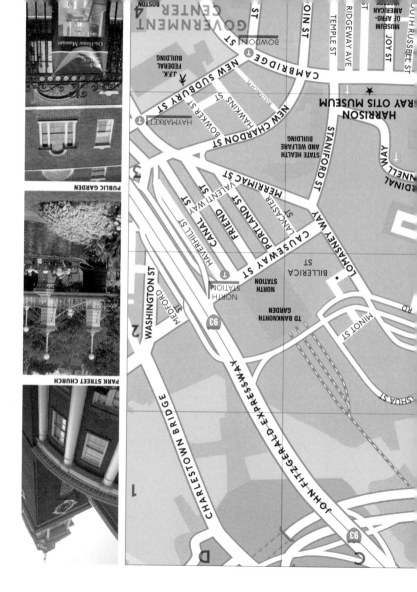

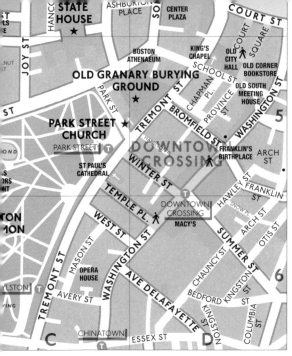

OLD GRANARY BURYING GROUND

ESPLANADE AND HATCH SHELL

chusetts Avenue
s, this popular park
gging paths, lagoons,
community sailing
. From spring to fall,
tch Shell hosts
or performances,
ost famous being
ston Pops Fourth
celebration. Each
housands of people
early in the morning
g prime patches of
for the concert and
rks display.

Street Church (B C5**)**
rk St
7) 523-3383
services 8.30am,
4pm and 6pm
miliar landmark grew
a controversial

'Religious Improvement
Society', safeguarded a
stash of gunpowder during
the War of 1812, and was
the site of William Lloyd
Garrison's first anti-slavery
speech. During the 19th
century, the church's 217-
foot steeple was the first
thing visitors saw when
approaching the city.

**Old Granary Burying
Ground (B** C-D5**)**
→ Tremont and Bromfield sts
This small but historically
rich cemetery dating from
1660 is a popular Freedom
Trail stop. Ornate
headstones mark the
graves of the giants of
American Revolutionary
history, including John

Hancock, Paul Revere and
Samuel Adams. The victims
of the 1770 Boston
Massacre are also here.

**Harrison Gray Otis
Museum (B** C4**)**
→ 141 Cambridge St
Tel. (617) 227-3956
Wed-Sun 11am–4.30pm.
www.historicnewengland.org
Enter the rarified world of
a Boston Brahmin in this
mansion designed by
Charles Bulfinch. Harrison
Gray Otis was a successful
lawyer and politician who
briefly served as mayor of
Boston. The interior has
been painstakingly restored
down to the lavish 18th-
and 19th-century furnishings
and vibrant colors.

**Museum of
Science (B** A-B2**)**
→ One Science Park
Tel. (617) 723-2500
Daily 9am–5pm (9pm Fri).
www.mos.org
This complex of science-
themed attractions has
three major traveling
exhibitions each year in
addition to the permanent
550 interactive ones.
Don't miss the lightning
demos, a full-size T. rex
model, and an interactive
archaeological dig.
You can explore outer space
at the Charles Hayden
Planetarium or dive into
the action with the Mugar
Omni Theater's five-story
IMAX screen.

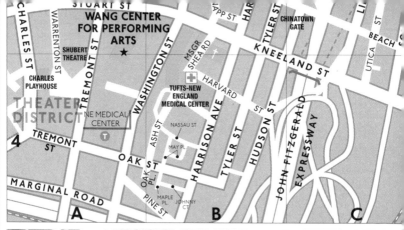

OLD CORNER BOOKSTORE

WANG CENTER FOR PERFORMING ARTS

NORMAN B. LEVE

Children's Museum (C F3)

→ 300 Congress St
Tel. (617) 426-8855
Daily 10am–5pm (9pm Fri)
www.bostonkids.org
Appropriately located next to the whimsical 40-foot Hood Milk Bottle, this museum is four stories of pint-sized interactive exhibits. Children can learn to rock climb, participate in a mini theater production and play dress-up in 'Grandparents' Attic'. Best of all, everything is educational, even the two-story climbing maze.

Opera House (C B2)

→ 539 Washington St
Tel. (617) 259-3400

Built in 1928 to showcase vaudeville acts, this Beaux-Arts building went through stints as a movie theater, a concert hall and an opera house. The theater began to decline after the Boston Opera Company collapsed in 1978, but was saved by a $38 million makeover in 2004. The gleaming venue reopened with *The Lion King*.

Boston Harborwalk (C D3-E2)

→ Tel. (617) 481-1722
www.bostonharborwalk.com
In an effort to reclaim the city's waterfront, a 46.9-mile public walkway is being constructed between Chelsea Creek and the

Neponset River. The Fort Point Channel has beautifully landscaped green spaces and prime views of the harbor and skyline. Grab a snack at the 40-foot Hood Milk Bottle or get a bird's-eye view at the 14th-floor observatory at 470 Atlantic Ave.

Chinatown (C B-C3)

The handful of streets that make up this lively neighborhood are densely packed with bakeries that double as roasted meat markets, grocers selling vacuum-packed eel and restaurants with live fish tanks in their windows. In recent years, Vietnamese,

Korean and Thai businesses have adde the cultural mix, and t area offers some of the city's most authentic ethnic fare.

Old South Meeting House (C C1)

→ 310 Washington St
Tel. (617) 482-6439
Daily 9.30am–5pm
(10am–4pm Nov-March)
A popular meeting spa during the American Revolution, this buildi famous for being the s of the 1777 protest tha inspired the Boston Te Party. Interactive exhib help visitors relive its history as a place of public debate.

c

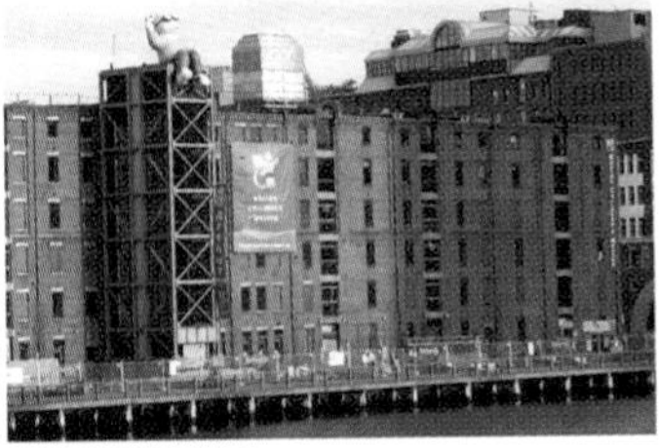

CHINATOWN

CENTRAL BURYING GROUND

BOYLSTON ST
BOYLSTON PL
BOYLSTON PL

CHINATOWN

TAMWORTH

BOYLSTON

ESSEX ST

PHILLIPS SQ

AVERY ST

TREMONT ST

BOYLSTON

WASHINGTON ST

AVE DE LAFAYETTE

BOYLSTON ST

OPERA HOUSE

MASON ST

WEST ST

BOSTON COMMON

SOLDIERS AND SAILORS MONUMENT

MACY'S

DOWNTOWN CROSSING

TEMPLE PLACE

FROG POND

ST PAUL'S CATHEDRAL

DOWNTOWN CROSSING

WINTER ST

PARK STREET

HAMILTON PL

ORPHEUM THEATRE

TREMONT ST

BEACON ST

FRANKLIN'S BIRTHPLACE

PROVINCE ST

BROMFIELD ST

PARK STREET CHURCH

OLD GRANARY BURYING GROUND

WALNUT ST

JOY ST

CHAPMAN PLACE

PROVINCE

SCHOOL ST

BOSTON ATHENAEUM

BOWDOIN ST

STATE HOUSE

MASSACHUSETTS STATE HOUSE

HANCOCK ST

CHESTNUT ST

OLD CITY HALL

KING'S CHAPEL

SOMERSET ST

VERNON ST

DAUGHTER HOUSES

OLD COR

CENTER PLAZA

PINCKNEY ST

NICHOLS HOUSE

COURT SQUARE

COURT

A

B

C

1

2

CHILDREN'S MUSEUM

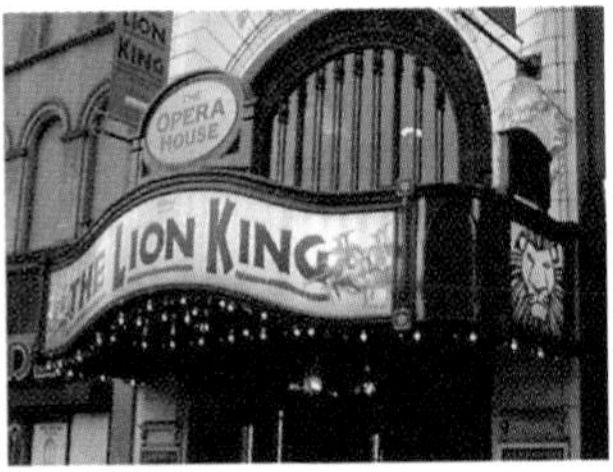

OPERA HOUSE

BOSTON HARBORW

THE LION KING

OPERA HOUSE

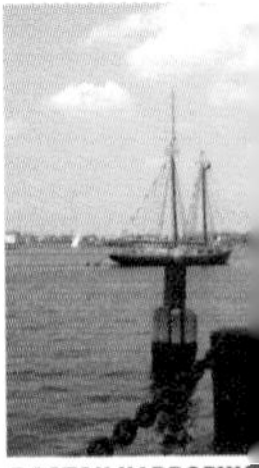

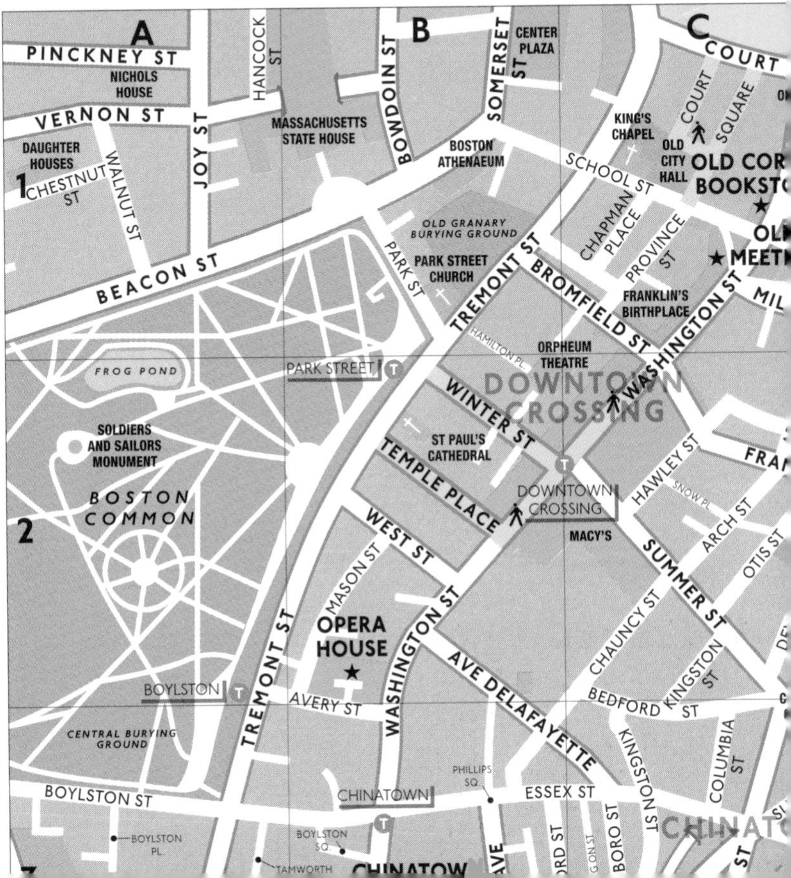

Just off Boston Common, Tremont Street becomes the Theater District, a cluster of major performance venues and a lively area after dark. A few blocks over, Chinatown is a sensory carnival – the chatter of Mandarin, the smell of roast duck, and the sight of exotic vegetables. Waves of immigrants have enriched this cultural mix, and the addition of authentic Vietnamese, Korean and Japanese restaurants makes this a dining destination. Bargain hunters flock to nearby Downtown Crossing, while the Financial District is finally loosening up, with new chic restaurants and bars. The ongoing Harbor Walk project promises to make the waterfront more accessible, with its great views and sights.

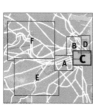

CHINA PEARL

RADIUS

RESTAURANTS

China Pearl (**C** B3)
→ *9 Tyler St*
Tel. (617) 426-4338
Daily 8.30am–11pm
On weekends, the mirrored staircase up to this second-floor dim sum palace is packed with customers who love the authentic dumplings and buns. Carts carrying chicken feet, steamed barbequed pork and egg custard tarts circle the room. Dim sum around $4 per piece.

The Barking Crab (**C** F3)
→ *88 Sleeper St*
Tel. (617) 426-2722
Daily 11.30am–11pm
(1am Thu-Sat)
It's summer all year round at this waterfront seafood shack, where mini lobster traps dangle above weathered picnic tables and Jimmy Buffet plays on repeat. Good crab cakes and chowder, and a million-dollar view of downtown Boston. Live music on Sun.
À la carte $18.

Mantra (**C** B2)
→ *52 Temple Place*
Tel. (617) 542-8111 Mon-Fri 11.30am–3pm, 5.30–10.30pm; Sat 5.30–10.30pm
Chainmail curtains and a 30-foot curved wooden

installation-cum-private alcove set the tone at this avant-garde French-Indian restaurant, and one of the city's hippest lounges.

Ginza (**C** C3)
→ *16 Hudson St*
Tel. (617) 338-2261
Daily 11.30am–2.30pm (4pm Sat-Sun), 5pm–2am (4am Tue-Sat)
Sushi connoisseurs come here for the deliciously fresh fish. Waitresses in kimonos present glistening pieces of sashimi, as well as the more unusual spider maki, made with soft-shelled crab, avocado and roe. Popular late-night hangout. À la carte $30.

Teatro (**C** A3)
→ *177 Tremont St*
Tel. (617) 778-6841 Mon-Sat 5pm–midnight; Sun 4–11pm
A dramatic 15-foot vaulted ceiling rises over the scene at this former synagogue. The lively atmosphere attracts a flashy crowd, as well as fashionable theater goers. Excellent thin-crust pizzas and generous portions of designer Italian fare. Can get very noisy.
À la carte $30.

Radius (**C** D2)
→ *8 High St*
Tel. (617) 426-1234 Mon-Fri 11.30am–2.30pm, 5.30–10p (11pm Fri); Sat 5.30pm–11pm
With many awards to its

ARKING CRAB **PEKING TOM'S** **BRATTLE BOOKSHOP**

name, chef Michael Schlow's popular temple of gastronomy leads the city's gourmet scene. Don't miss the roasted arctic char with melted leeks, artichokes and pickled ramps or the huckleberry cheesecake. Tasting menus are worth the price. À la carte $55.

Spire (C B1)
→ 90 Tremont St
Tel. (617) 772-0202
Mon-Fri 6.30–10.30am, 11.30am–2pm, 5.30–10pm; Sat- Sun 8am–2pm, 5.30–10pm (9.30pm Sun)
Clean design and flawless service characterize this popular spot where former Radius chef Gabriel Frasca cooks up intricate but playful French food: try the diver scallops with a bay scallop Bloody Mary and carrot-cumin soup or the black mission fig tart topped with rosemary ice cream. À la carte $55.

BARS, CAFÉS, NIGHTCLUBS

Apollo Grill & Sushi Restaurant (C B3)
→ 84 Harrison Ave
Tel. (617) 423-3888 Daily 11.30am–2.30pm, 5pm–4am
Pesky blue laws shut Boston clubs down at 2am, but the party

continues at this nondescript Chinatown restaurant. Hip kids nosh on Korean barbeque and California rolls, and the Sapporo flows like water into the wee hours.

Caprice (C A4)
→ 275 Tremont St
Tel. (617) 292-0080
Mon-Tue 10pm–2am; Wed-Sun 5pm–2am
The Euro-heavy first-floor restaurant and bar are especially busy pre-theater, but the sultry second-floor lounge heats up after midnight. Full menu of Mediterranean and French dishes available until 12.30am.

Peking Tom's (C C2)
→ 25 Kingston St
Tel. (617) 482-6282
Mon-Sat 11.30am–2am; Sun 5.30pm–2am
Creative cocktails and a sensual Far East aesthetic attract a crowd of well-off 20-somethings. Upscale takeout includes crab Rangoon, potstickers, scallion pancakes – until 1am.

Aria (C A3)
→ 246 Tremont St
Tel (617) 338-7080
Tue, Thu-Su 11pm–2am
A modestly sized club patronized by a well-heeled set. Mainstream hip hop inspires a good

amount of bumping and grinding on the dance floor, while buying bottles of Cristal will get you VIP treatment. Cover around $15.

Gypsy Bar (C A3)
→ 116 Boylston St
Tel. (617) 482-7799
Tue-Sat 5.30pm–2am
Fuchsia fish float in glowing tanks, lending a otherworldly vibe to this sleekly trendy club. Strict dress code, but most of the well-dressed clientele wouldn't dream of wearing sneakers anyway. Cover around $10.

THEATERS

Wang Theater (C A4)
→ 270 Tremont St
Tel. (617) 482-9393
Box office: daily 10am–6pm
An architectural landmark and benchmark for Boston Theater. Hosts everything from Boston Ballet to the Foo Fighters to the Radio City Christmas Spectacular.

Shubert Theater (C A4)
→ 265 Tremont St
Tel. (617) 482-9393
Box office: daily 10am–6pm
The Theater District's 'Little Princess', this 1600-seat palace stages national Broadway shows, including the enormously popular Rent.

SHOPPING

Brattle Bookshop (C B2)
→ 9 West St
Tel. (617) 542-0210
Mon-Sat 9am–5.30pm
Tucked down a tiny side street amid mass-market discount shops, this three-story bookstore is one of Boston's oldest. Stacks and tables brim with maps, books, prints and magazines, and owner Ken Gloss has also amassed an impressive collection of rare and first edition books.

Van's Fabrics (C B3)
→ 14 Beach St
Tel. (617) 423-6592
Daily 10.30am–6pm
Clued-in seamstresses and decorators come here for the huge array of gorgeous silks, embroidered fabrics, inexpensive bright cloth and Buddha figurines.

Boston Costume (C B3)
→ 69 Kneeland St, Suite 1
Tel. (617) 482-1632
Mon-Sat 9.30am–6pm
A mind-boggling array of costumes and accessories. Rent a full latex Batman suit or invest in a deluxe Chewbacca mask. This is the go-to store for local film, television, and theater companies.

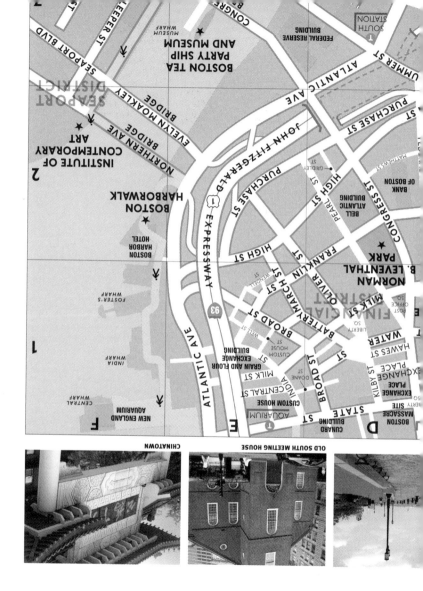

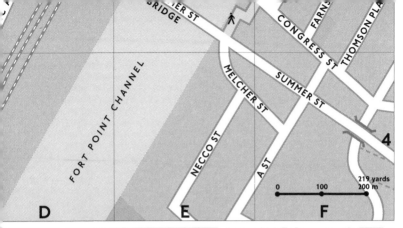

D · **E** · **F**

FORT POINT CHANNEL

BRIDGE

CONGRESS ST · FARNS · THOMSON PLA

MELCHER ST · SUMMER ST

NECCO ST · A ST

4

| 0 | 100 | 200 m |

219 yards

INSTITUTE OF CONTEMPORARY ART

BOSTON TEA PARTY SHIP

orner
store (C C1)
School St (corner of
ngton and School sts)
dest 1712 building
a sterling literary
age: Some of the 19th
ry's most celebrated
rs, including Ralph
o Emerson and Henry
worth Longfellow,
published by Ticknor
ds, which had offices
from 1832–65.
g Center for
orming Arts (C A3)
→ *8 Tremont St*
17) 482-9393
wangcenter.org
its heyday in the
ng 20s, the lavish
-illes-inspired

Metropolitan Theater fell
into disrepair. In 1983,
Dr An Wang made a
generous donation that
stimulated a massive
$9.8 million renovation.
With the marble columns
and gilt-edged mirrors
gleaming once again, the
renamed Wang Center
opened as the city's premier
Broadway venue and the
home of the Boston Ballet.
Norman B. Leventhal
Park (C D2)
→ *Between Pearl and*
Congress sts
A rare swath of green in the
sterile Financial District,
this park is often cited as
an example of good urban
planning. A ramshackle

parking garage (which
now funds the project) was
moved below ground to
make room for the park's
restaurant, fountains,
outdoor art and 125
varieties of plants.
Institute of
Contemporary Art (C F2)
→ *Fan Pier*
Tel. (617) 266-5152 Tue-Sun
10am–5pm (9pm Thu-Fri)
www.icaboston.org
Diller Scofidio and Renfro
have designed the city's
only exclusively modern
art museum: 65,000
square feet, part of which is
cantilevered over Boston
Harbor. ICA has long
cultivated up-and-coming
artists, including Andy

Warhol and Cindy Sherman,
and will now be able to
develop a permanent
collection. Also in the new
building are a media center,
a two-story education
center and a performing
arts theater.
Boston Tea Party Ship
and Museum (C E3)
→ *Congress Street Bridge*
www.bostonteapartyship.
com
A fire forced the closing of
the site of the famous
act of rebellion, but a new
museum is going to open
in late 2007. Two new tall
ships will join the replica
of the *Brig Beaver* already
in the harbor. All three will
be open for tours.

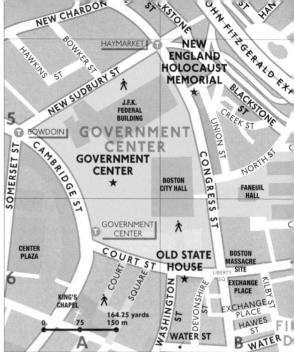

NEW ENGLAND AQUARIUM

NEW ENGLAND AQUARIUM

Map labels:
NEW CHARDON ST · BLACKSTONE ST · JOHN F. FITZGERALD EX · HAN · HAYMARKET · NEW ENGLAND HOLOCAUST MEMORIAL · BOWKER ST · HAWKINS ST · NEW SUDBURY ST · J.F.K. FEDERAL BUILDING · CREEK ST · BLACKSTONE ST · BOWDOIN · CAMBRIDGE ST · SOMERSET ST · UNION ST · NORTH ST · GOVERNMENT CENTER · GOVERNMENT CENTER · BOSTON CITY HALL · FANEUIL HALL · CONGRESS ST · GOVERNMENT CENTER · CENTER PLAZA · COURT ST · OLD STATE HOUSE · BOSTON MASSACRE SITE · LIBERTY SQ · EXCHANGE PLACE · KILBY ST · COURT SQUARE · KING'S CHAPEL · 164.25 yards · 150 m · 0 · 75 · WASHINGTON ST · DEVONSHIRE ST · EXCHANGE PLACE · HAWES ST · WATER ST · FI · A · B · WATER

5 **6** **A** **B**

Old North Church (**D** C3)
→ 193 Salem St
Tel. (617) 523-6676
Daily 9am–5pm
This classical church in the Christopher Wren style was where the American Revolution really began. On April 18, 1775, sexton Robert Newman shimmied up the steeple to hang the two lanterns that signaled Paul Revere to begin his ride.

Paul Revere House (**D** C4)
→ 19 North Square
Tel. (617) 523-2338
Daily, mid-April-Oct: 9.30am–5.15pm; Nov-mid-April: 9.30am–4.15pm
The famous Revolutionary War hero once lived in this simple 1680 two-story

clapboard house. None of Revere's furniture remains, but the house has been carefully designed to mimic early colonial living arrangements.

Copp's Hill Burying Ground (**D** B2)
→ Hull St
Worth a visit for the view alone, this cemetery occupies an elevated parcel of land overlooking the Charles River. During the Battle of Bunker Hill, the British turned this to their advantage, firing cannons from here at Charlestown. Most of the graves belong to North End merchants and artisans, with the exception of Puritan conservatives

Cotton Mather and his father, Increase.

Old State House (**D** B6)
→ 206 Washington St
Tel. (617) 720-1713
Daily 9.30am–5pm
A colonial reminder amid a forest of skyscrapers, this dignified 1713 edifice is Boston's oldest public building. The Declaration of Independence was read from its balcony, and nearby a plaque marks the site of the 1770 Boston Massacre. On display are John Hancock's coat, and tea from the Boston Tea Party. The 'Colony to Commonwealth' permanent exhibit of images and artifacts, on the first floor,

is a tidy crash course Massachusetts's histo

New England Aquarium (**D** D6)
→ Central Wharf
Tel. (617) 973-5200 Dai 9am–5pm (6pm Sat-Sur IMAX: daily 9.30am–9.3
Relatively small but pa with attractions, this aquarium revolves arc three-story, 200,000-g saltwater tank teemin everything from sea tu to sharks. A winding walkway lets you trave the bottom of the 'oce floor' to the surface (tr catch a feeding sessio Also daily sea lion sho seasonal whale watch tours, and an IMAX th

MORTO
STILLMAN ST
VALENTI WAY
SALEM ST
WIGET ST
PARM
PL.
BALDWIN PL.
ST BARTLETT PL.
NOYES PL.
NORTH MARGIN ST
COOPER
ST
LYNN ST
THACHER ST
PORTLAND
FRIEND ST
CANAL ST
HAVERHILL ST
93
PRINCE
PRINCE ST
MARGARET ST
SHEAFE S
SNOWHILL ST
ENDICOTT ST
MARGIN ST
WASHINGTON ST
MEDFORD ST
NORTH STATION
NORTH STATION
CAUSEWAY ST
HULL ST
COPP'S HILL ★ BURYING GROUND
COMMER
CHA
JOHN FITZGERALD EXPRESSWAY
3
CHARLESTOWN BRIDGE
N WASHINGTON ST
2
CONSTITUTION RD
CHARLESTOWN ST
CHELSEA ST
CITY SQ.
BUNKER HILL PAVILION
BUNKER HILL MONUMENT ★ ↓
USS CONSTITU (OLD IRONSI AND MUSEU
B ★

1

A

North End / Waterfront

COPP'S HILL BURYING GROUND

OLD NORTH CHURCH

Many of Boston's key historical sites lie along the portion of the Freedom Trail between Government Center and the waterfront. Despite its engineered kitschiness, Faneuil Hall is an impressive testament to the city's controversial past, and the attached Quincy Market is a fun way to pass a few hours. For years, the city's infamous Big Dig separated the North End from downtown. With the end of major construction at the beginning of 2006, this vibrant Italian enclave is more popular than ever: budding chefs source their imported pastas and cheese; visitors seek out the city's best gnocchi; and locals come for the cannoli and espresso. The city's oldest neighborhood, it is also the site of seminal moments in American history.

MODERN PASTRY

LUCCA

RESTAURANTS

Pizzeria Regina (D B3)
→ 11 1/2 Thacher St
Tel. (617) 227-0765 Daily
11am (noon Sun)–11pm
Crisp, lightly charred crusts and fresh tomato sauce elevate this pie – the first and still the best of all the offshoots – above the pack. Pizzas around $10.

Union Oyster House (D B5)
→ 41 Union St
Tel. (617) 227-2750 Daily
11am–9.30pm (10pm Fri-Sat)
The country's oldest restaurant has been serving steamers and chowder since 1826. Have a look at John F. Kennedy's favorite second-floor booth. À la carte $30.

Neptune Oyster Bar (D B4)
→ 63 Salem St
Tel. (617) 742-3474
Daily 11.30am–11pm
There is a marble bar and stylish European decor, and Boston tastemakers come here for light, greaseless fried clams, oyster po'boys and lobster rolls (either hot with butter or cold with mayo). À la carte $30.

Legal Seafoods (D C6)
→ 255 State St
Tel. (617) 227-3919 Daily
11am (noon Sun)–11pm
What began as a Cambridge fish market is now a local institution with more than 30 branches along the East Coast. Despite the uninspired decor the seafood is first-rate; try the clambake followed by Boston cream pie. À la carte $35.

Lucca (D B4)
→ 226 Hanover St
Tel. (617) 742-9200
Daily 11.30am–1am
This elegant Italian restaurant with soft lighting and discreet service has an original menu that includes roasted duck tart with caramelized onions and goat cheese and fresh rigatoni with braised wild boar ragù. À la carte $40.

Bricco (D B4)
→ 241 Hanover St
Tel. (617) 248-6800
Daily 5pm–2am
A North End favorite with an excellent reputation and sky-high prices to match. The elaborate Italian dishes use ingredients of the highest quality: black truffles, imported Speck, kobe beef. Snag a table near the huge windows so you can take in the bustling Hanover Street scene over espresso and deep, dark Valrhona chocolate cake. À la carte $50.

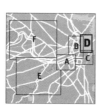

L SEAFOODS

IN JEAN LUS

CHEERS

BARS, MUSIC VENUE

Café Vittoria (D C4)
→ 296 Hanover St
Tel. (617) 227-7606
Daily 8am–1am
This often crowded café has lots of atmosphere and makes a perfect espresso.

The Living Room (D C5)
→ 101 Atlantic Ave
Tel. (617) 723-5101 Daily 11.30am (10am Sun)–1am
Cushy sofas and sheer purple curtains make this lounge feel more like an apartment. Clean-cut investment bankers from the nearby Financial District convene after hours around classic martinis and elaborate bar food.

Cheers (D B5)
→ South Canopy, Quincy Market. Tel. (617) 227-0150
Daily 11am–2am
Fans of the long-running show may grumble about authenticity (the real Cheers is a nondescript bar in Beacon Hill), but this kitsch watering hole is a fun place to refuel after serious sightseeing.

The Purple Shamrock (D B5)
→ 1 Union St
Tel. (617) 227-2060 Daily 11.30am (11am Sun)–2am
A slightly dingy but lovable Irish bar on the outskirts of Faneuil Hall, it attracts a young, casual crowd and college kids at the weekend. Tuesday is karaoke night, and there are frequent performances by local rock bands.

SHOPPING

In Jean Lus (D C3)
→ 441 Hanover St
Tel. (617) 523-5326 Mon-Fri 11am–8pm; Sat 10am–7pm; Sun noon–6pm
This high-end denim shop is a welcome addition to the boutique-deprived North End. All the usual suspects are here – Citizens of Humanity, Hudson, and Joe's.

Salumeria Italiana (D C4)
→ 151 Richmond St
Tel. (617) 400-5916
Mon-Sat 8am–6pm
When this North End grocer opened in 1962, it was the only place in the city to get extra-virgin olive oil. Although that's no longer the case, connoisseurs still line up for fresh white and black truffles flown in from Italy, bottarga di tonno and aged balsamic vinegar.

Modern Pastry (D C4)
→ 257 Hanover St
Tel. (617) 523-3783

Daily 8am–10pm
When the lines at Mike's Pastry twist out the door, locals head across the street to this cozy family-owned shop. Crisp cannoli shells are filled to order with fresh ricotta, and there is also a vast array of Italian sweets and cookies, including the house specialty, honey almond nougat.

Dairy Fresh (D B4)
→ 57 Salem St
Tel. (617) 742-2639
Mon-Fri 9am–7pm; Sat 8am–7pm; Sun 11pm–6pm
Packed with jewel-toned candied fruits, aromatic roasted nuts and decadent bricks of fudge, this tiny shop brings out the child in everyone. Cooks will love the selection of Valrhona baking chocolate, Bensdorp cocoa, and imported extracts.

Shake the Tree Gallery (D B4)
→ 95 Salem St
Tel. (617) 742-0484
Mon-Fri 11am–7pm (6pm Mon-Tue; 8.30pm Fri); Sat 10am–9pm; Sun noon–6pm
A departure from the usual grocers and cafés of the food-centric North End, this trendy boutique has great gifts: Red Flower beauty products, glossy cookbooks and buttery Tano bags. The small but terrific clothes section includes frocks by Shoshanna and Plenty and supersoft velvet tees.

Faneuil Hall and Quincy Market (D B5)
→ Faneuil Hall, 15 State St
Daily 9am–5pm
www.faneuilhallmarketplace.com
→ Quincy Market, Chatham and Quincy sts
Mon-Sat 10am–9pm; Sun noon–6pm
This Disneyesque restaurant and shopping complex is worth seeing once. Faneuil Hall, once a colonial meetinghouse, now mostly hosts souvenir stalls, while Quincy Market is one long food court, flanked on both sides by kiosks selling all manner of knickknacks. Both are home to 100 or so major retailers such as Swatch, Orvis, Crate & Barrel and Urban Outfitters.

Bostonian Society Museum Shop
→ South Canopy, Quincy Market. Tel. (617) 720-3284
Daily 10am–6pm
A great place to pick up souvenirs inspired by the Revolutionary Era – or just stock up on saltwater taffy.

GOVERNMENT CENTER

OLD STATE HOUSE

BOSTON INNER HARBOR

USS CASSIN YOUNG

ATLANTIC AVE

SARGENT WHARF

UNION WHARF

LINCOLN WHARF

BATTERY WHARF

CONSTITUTION WHARF

CALLAHAN TRAFFIC TUNNEL

SUMNER TRAFFIC TUNNEL

MOON ST

SACRED HEART [?]

TONY DE MARCO WAY

PAUL REVERE HOUSE

GARDEN COURT ST

NORTH ST

HANOVER ST

CLARK ST

HARRIS ST

HANOVER AVE

SALUTATION ST

BATTERY ST

CHARTER ST

GREENHOUGH LANE

HENCHMAN ST

FOSTER ST

UNITY ST

TILESTON ST

HANOVER PARK AND GARDENS

TARNET ST

4

3

2

1

A

B

C

D

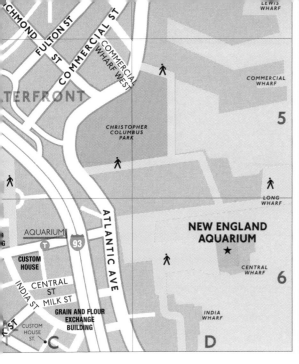

USS *CONSTITUTION*

CHRISTOPHER COLUMBUS PARK

COMMERCIAL WHARF

COMMERCIAL WHARF WEST

LEWIS WHARF

WATERFRONT

LONG WHARF

NEW ENGLAND AQUARIUM ★

CENTRAL WHARF

INDIA WHARF

AQUARIUM

CUSTOM HOUSE

CENTRAL ST

MILK ST

INDIA ST

GRAIN AND FLOUR EXCHANGE BUILDING

CUSTOM HOUSE ST.

ATLANTIC AVE

RICHMOND ST

FULTON ST

COMMERCIAL ST

COMMERCIAL WHARF

93

C

D

5

6

BUNKER HILL MONUMENT

Constitution and ...eum (D B1)
...arlestown Navy Yard
...517) 242-7511
...un 10am–5.50pm
...Sun 10am–3.50pm
...March). Last tour
...ins before closing time.
...um: daily 9am–6pm
...n–5pm Nov–April)
...g the Battle of 1812,
...wooden warship was
...fective at repelling
...ed the cannons that it
...ed the nickname 'Old
...ides'. The world's
...st commissioned
...hip afloat, she has
... scrupulously
...tained. Active-duty
...Navy sailors in period
...umes lead 30- to 40-

minute tours that are often
as entertaining as they are
informative. The adjacent
museum aims to bring
'Ironsides' alive through
hands-on exhibits and
maritime artifacts.
**New England Holocaust
Memorial (D B5)**
→ Carmen Park, on Congress
Street near Faneuil Hall
Tel. (617) 457-8755
Despite the physical
proximity, Stanley
Saitowitz's lyrical memorial
feels far from the tumult of
Faneuil Hall. To experience
the exhibit, you follow
a black granite path
through six 54-foot
glass structures, each set
above a dark chamber

symbolizing the main
concentration camps. Six
million numbers etched on
the walls are a horrific
reminder of the human
cost of the Holocaust.
Bunker Hill Monument
(Off map, north of A1)
→ Tel. (617) 242-5641
Daily 9am–4.30pm
It was here that William
Prescott famously ordered
an outnumbered rebel
army, 'Don't fire until you
see the whites of their
eyes!' The bloody battle
that followed proved to
be the turning point in the
Revolutionary War and is
commemorated by a
221-foot granite obelisk.
It's worth climbing the

294 steps to the top of the
monument for a bird's-eye
view of the city and harbor.
**Government
Center (D A5)**
→ City Hall and
City Hall Plaza
The Government Center
(designed by I. M. Pei)
was meant to revitalize the
Scollay Square area, but
the 1960s renewal project
is widely regarded as a
failure. The 8-acre City Hall
Plaza, devoid of green
space, has a sterile feel,
which is only exacerbated
by the Brutalist behemoth
of City Hall. Unless there is
a festival or concert, the
plaza's main traffic is
government employees.

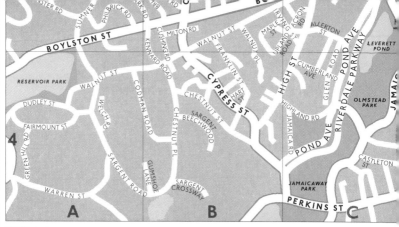

Map with labels: BOYLSTON ST, RESERVOIR PARK, WALNUT ST, DUDLEY ST, FAIRMOUNT ST, WARREN ST, SARGENT ROAD, GUMSHOE LANE, SARGENT CROSSWAY, CODMAN ROAD, WELCH RD, GREEN HILL RD, CHESTNUT ST, CHESTNUT PL, SARGENT BEECHWOOD, CYPRESS ST, HART ST, MILTON RD, WALNUT ST, CUSHING RD, KENNARD ROAD, FRANKLIN ST, MAPLE ST, IRVING ST, ACTON ST, HIGH ST, CUMBERLAND AVE, GLEN ROAD, JAMAICA RD, POND AVE, RIVERDALE PARKWAY, POND AVE, LEVERETT POND, OLMSTEAD PARK, CASTLETON ST, JAMAICAWAY PARK, JAMAICAWAY, PERKINS ST, HIGHLAND RD, ALLERTON ST

A   B   C

4

KENNEDY NATIONAL HISTORICAL SITE

COOLIDGE CORNER THEATER

COOLIDGE CORNER

Fenway Park (E E1)
→ Tel. (877) 733-7699 (tickets)
Tel. (617) 226-6666
Tours daily 9am–4pm
Boston Red Sox fans have been called masochistic, manic-depressive, and fanatical. Members of Red Sox Nation are proud of their obsession: they have a mythology, the Curse of the Bambino; an anthem, 'Sweet Caroline'; and, of course, a temple, Fenway Park. It's worth the price of admission: there are decent views from even the cheapest seats and the enthusiasm of Sox fans is infectious. While always rowdy on game days, nothing will top October 27,

2004, when the team broke its 86-year-long losing streak. Rock concerts also go on here.

Museum of Fine Arts (E E2)
→ 465 Huntington Ave
Tel. (617) 267-9300
Daily 10am–4.45pm (9.45pm Wed-Fri). www.mfa.org
One of the largest museums in the US, this sprawling neoclassical structure houses an encyclopedic collection of more than 450,000 objects; it is known for its Egyptian artifacts, impressionist works by Gauguin, Manet, Degas and Monet as well as 19th-century art including Sargent. There is also the

Morse collection of Japanese pottery. Currently under massive renovation, the museum will add 151,000 square feet by 2010, catapulting it into the 21st century in terms of architecture and facilities.

Isabella Stewart Gardner Museum (E E2)
→ 280 The Fenway
Tel. (617) 566-1401
Tue-Sun 11am–5pm.
www.gardnermuseum.org
Avid art patron and globetrotter Isabella Stewart Gardner founded this museum in 1903 to showcase her Berenson-edited collection of painting, sculpture and decorative arts, including

works by Rembrandt, Botticelli, Titian and Vermeer. Inspired by a century Venetian palaz the building has three stories of galleries surrounding a beautifu planted garden court. Café, overlooking thes gardens, is known for incredible desserts an transporting setting. The famous 1990 robb has left 13 blank space on the walls.

Back Bay Fens (E E-Fr
Frederick Law Olmsted responsible for New Yc Central Park, spent 20 creating Boston's 'Eme Necklace'. The string o green spaces includes

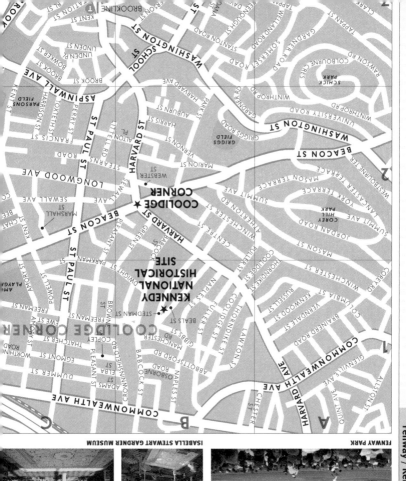

ISABELLA STEWART GARDNER MUSEUM

FENWAY PARK

To the southeast of Back Bay, the often-neglected Back Bay Fens is part of Frederick Law Olmsted's lovely Emerald Necklace, a succession of green spaces throughout the city. The Fens sits between cultural extremes: to the south lie two exceptional art museums, while to the north is Kenmore Square, a sea of baseball caps and pennants. The heart of the latter, and its claim to fame, is Fenway Park. The neon Citgo sign looming overhead is a beacon for members of Red Sox Nation, who turn the streets into a block party during baseball season. A few T stops farther out, Brookline is a pleasant residential area with unique shops and restaurants.

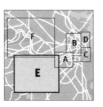

CASK N' FLAGON

BOSTON BILLIARD CLUB

RESTAURANTS

El Pelon Taqueria (E E2)
→ 92 Peterborough St
Tel. (617) 262-9090
Daily 11.30am–11pm
A favorite of Fenway-area students for its fresh, full-flavored Mexican food and rock-bottom prices. Sides such as limed onions, salsa fresca and crema (Mexican crème fraiche) propel the tacos and burritos into gourmet territory. Excellent horchata, a traditional rice-based drink flavored with cinnamon and almonds. À la carte $4.
If Beacon St is closer, **Anna's Taqueria**, at no. 1412 (**E** B2), is another favorite.

Zaftigs (E B2)
→ 335 Harvard St
Tel. (617) 975-0075
Daily 8am–10pm
Massive portions of updated Jewish favorites: Israeli couscous salad is studded with fennel, dried cranberries and walnuts, and granola pancakes come with tangy date butter. À la carte $15.

Petit Robert Bistro (E E1)
→ 468 Commonwealth Ave
Tel. (617) 375-0699
Daily 11am–11pm
Chef Jacky Robert infuses

the fast food predominanc of Kenmore Square with a little Left Bank. Perfect bistro staples, such as soupe à l'oignon gratinée and roasted chicken, are delicious and gently price Delicate pastries include a gateau Petit Robert topped by a chocolate Eiffel Tower. À la carte $25

Elephant Walk (E D1)
→ 900 Beacon St
Tel. (617) 247-1500
Mon-Fri 11.30am–2.30pm, 5pm–10pm (11pm Fri); Sat-Sun 5pm–10pm (11pm Sat)
The menu of this sophisticated spot is divided into Cambodian and French dishes. The former are more interestin and include a silky smoot black cod glazed with soy garlic. À la carte $35.

Fugakyu (E C2)
→ 1280 Beacon St
Tel. (617) 734-1268
Mon-Sat 11.30am–1.30am; Sun noon–1.30am
The moat on the bar with boats bearing sushi give this spot a theme park air. The sashimi, including the coveted tuna belly, is deliciously fresh, and ther are plenty of non-raw options, plus fantastic tempura green tea ice cream. À la carte $35.

Great Bay (E E1)
→ 500 Commonwealth Ave

MURPHY'S PUB

YAWKEY WAY

MAGIC BEAN

Tel. (617) 532-5300 Daily
5–10pm (11pm Thu-Sat);
Sun 10am–2pm
Part of the Radius (see **C**)
group, this upscale
seafood restaurant and
raw bar is in the Hotel
Commonwealth. Try the
panko-crusted chatham
cod served with house-
made chorizo, cranberry
beans, sweet 100s, and
shrimp. À la carte $45.

BARS, ICE CREAM PARLOR, BILLIARDS

J.P. Licks (E B2)
→ *311 Harvard St*
Tel. (617) 738-8252
Daily 11am–midnight
Ice cream fanatics swear
by this local chain.
Cheerful cow-print murals
cover the walls, and
staff is happy to let you
sample flavors.
**Matt Murphy's
Pub (E** C3)
→ *14 Harvard St*
Tel. (617) 232-0188
Daily 11am–2am (1am Sat)
A gastro-pub before the
term was coined, this
neighborhood bar serves
better-than-homemade
renditions of Irish
favorites such as
shepherd's pie and pork
sausage. Nightly free
music, ranging from jazz
to folk, and quiz contests.

À la carte $15.
Cask n' Flagon (E E1)
→ *62 Brookline Ave*
Tel. (617) 536-4840 Daily
11.30am–1am (2am Thu-Sat)
Decorated with nostalgic
black-and-white photos of
Ted Williams and Babe
Ruth, this die-hard Red
Sox bar is as close to
Fenway as you can get
without a ticket. A gigantic
bar and 45" flat-screen
TVs make it one of the
area's most popular
game-watching spots.
**Boston Billiard
Club (E** E1)
→ *126 Brookline Ave*
Tel. (617) 536-7665
Daily noon–2am
This sprawling adult
funhouse has more than
50 pool tables, private
rooms and big screen
TVs and attracts young
professionals, although
things can get a little frat-
house rowdy during big
sports games.

NIGHTCLUB

Avalon (E E1)
→ *15 Lansdowne St*
Tel. (617) 262-2424 Thu-Sat
10pm–2am; Sun 9pm–2am
The city's largest club,
with a 2,000-dancer
capacity, high-tech light
system and oxygen bar.
The crowd varies: Sun is

gay-friendly while Thu
is reserved for Euros.
Weekends often bring
big-name guest DJs.
Cover around $15.

SHOPPING

Yawkey Way (E E1)
If you want to jump on
the Red Sox bandwagon,
this is the place to pick
up some red and blue
paraphernalia. Running
alongside Fenway Park,
this street becomes a
festive block party on
game days, complete with
food vendors, live music,
and local TV broadcasts.
Yawkey Way Store
→ *19 Yawkey Way*
Tel. (800) 336-9299
Daily 9am–5pm, extended
hours during home games
Magic Beans (E B2)
→ *312 Harvard St*
Tel. (617) 264-2326 Mon-Sat
10am–6pm (8pm Thu; 7pm
Fri-Sat); Sun 11am–5pm
This dynamic shop stocks
all the hottest trends in
baby gear, including high-
tech Stokke strollers, pink
camo diaper bags, and
Modernist high chairs.
Kids will love the toy
selection: spy kits, indoor
tents, doll houses, etc.
Jean Therapy (E E1)
→ *524 Commonwealth Ave*
Tel. (617) 266-6555

Mon-Sat 11am–7pm;
Sun noon–6pm
Under the Hotel
Commonwealth, this
shop specializes in such
upscale denim lines as
Paige Premium, Sacred
Blue, and Drifter. Owner
Leah Eckelberger makes
it her mission to find the
best blues for your bum,
even scheduling private
consultations.
**Brookline
Booksmith (E** B2)
→ *279 Harvard St*
Tel. (617) 566-6660
Mon-Fri 8.30am–10pm
(11 Fri); Sat 9am–11pm;
Sun 10am–8pm
Local bibliophiles love this
independent bookstore's
extensive inventory. The
amiable staff gives great
recommendations, and the
used book cellar has plenty
of low-priced gems.
Paper Source (E C2)
→ *1361 Beacon St*
Tel. (617) 264-2800
Mon-Sat 10am–7pm (6pm
Sat); Sun 11am–6pm
A vast emporium of colorful
stationery, elegant
bookbinding kits, and
tasteful knickknacks.
The Brookline outpost of
this stationer has a
knowledgeable staff that
can help you pick out a
hostess gift or design
your own calling card.

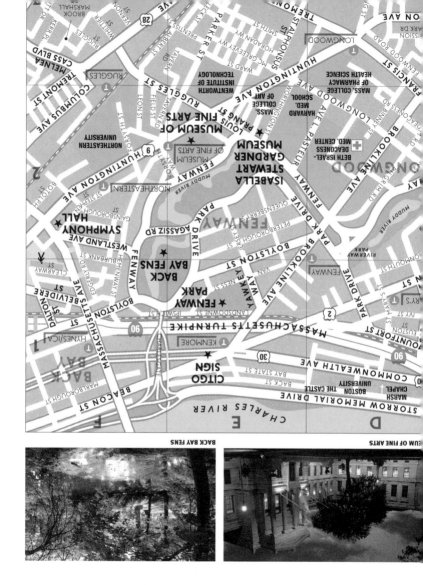

BACK BAY FENS

...EUM OF FINE ARTS

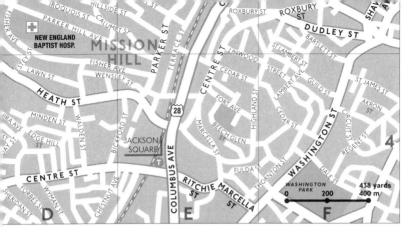

BOSTON SYMPHONY HALL

CITGO SIGN

...er toxic swamp, now ...sformed into a popular ... with splendid ...woods and a shady ...water lagoon. In spring, ...ames P. Kelleher Rose ...den is an explosion of ...r and fragrance, with ...-wreathed archways ... a central fountain. ...e: The park is not ... to wander around in ...r dark.

...go sign (E E1)
...he heart of Kenmore ...are, this iconic 60-by-...foot sign has become ...ntegral part of the city ...scape. At night, it ...inates the skyline with ...ulsing pattern of red, ...e, and blue. Because

of its conspicuous position over the left wall of Fenway Park, it has become entwined with Red Sox superstition. A 2005 upgrade replaced the outdated neon tubing with high-tech LED.

Coolidge Corner (E B2)
Just four miles and a short T ride outside Boston proper, the affluent suburb of Brookline is an idyllic escape. Coolidge Corner is an outdoor shopping area catering to a fashionable, unpretentious clientele. Here you'll find boutiques stocked with lux designer goods, baby stores with the latest hip mom gear, and gourmet candy shops. A

slice of 1930s glamour, the art-deco Coolidge Corner Theater shows independent movies, classic films and documentaries.

Kennedy National Historical Site (E B1)
→ 83 Beals St
Tel. (617) 566-7937
Wed–Sun 10am–4.30pm
Down a quiet Brookline street, the birthplace of America's 35th president resembles any other suburban home. When it was established as a memorial in 1967, Rose Kennedy directed the restoration to its original 1917 state, down to the furniture and photographs. Her audio tour of the house

strikes a very personal note.
Symphony Hall (E F2)
→ 301 Massachusetts Ave
Tel. (617) 266-1492
www.bso.org
Designed by the preeminent early-20th-century team of McKim, Mead and White, this 1900 Beaux-Arts building was the first to use scientific principles in order to create optimal acoustics. Today, even hard-to-please younger listeners can appreciate the catchy Boston Pops orchestra, conducted by Keith Lockhart. For a forceful Rachmaninov or Bach concerto, the Boston Symphony Orchestra is your ticket.

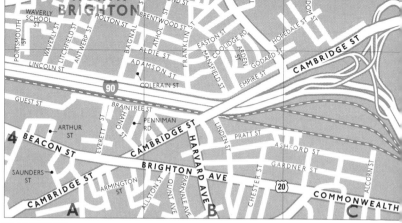

CHRIST CHURCH

STAIRS IN THE MIT MUSEUM AND SCULPTURES IN THE MIT GARDENS

Harvard University Art Museums (F D2)
→ Tel. (617) 495-9400
Daily 10am (1pm Sun)–5pm
Fogg Art Museum
→ 32 Quincy St
www.artmuseums.harvard.
edu/fogg
Harvard's oldest museum, with three floors of galleries, centered on a regal Renaissance courtyard, exhibits only a fraction of the university's priceless collection of Italian early Renaissance, British Pre-Raphaelite, impressionist and postimpressionist art. There is also a well-rounded collection of modern art featuring seminal works by

Jasper Johns and Frank Stella among others.
Arthur M. Sackler Museum
→ 485 Broadway
www.sackler.org
British architect Peter Stirling added this modern annex to the Fogg. The collection of Asian, Islamic, and Ancient art includes Chinese jade, 2nd-century statues and Japanese Surimono prints.
Busch-Reisinger Museum
→ www.artmuseums.
harvard.edu/busch
Werner Otto Hall, located on Prescott Street and accessible via the second floor of the Fogg, is a small but comprehensive museum dedicated to

Germanic art. Permanent exhibits highlight works from postwar abstract artists such as Wassily Kandinsky and Paul Klee, and the museum's impressive Joseph Beuys collection.
Harvard University (F C2)
→ Tel. (617) 495-1000
Founded in 1636, Harvard is the country's oldest school of higher education. The university is vast, but most people opt to tour the grounds of Harvard College. Highlights include picturesque Harvard Yard, bordered by ivy-covered brick dormitories; Widener Library, with 50 miles of shelves; and the John

Harvard statue, known f its lucky toe.
Ray and Maria Stata Center, MIT (F F3)
→ 32 Vassar St
Tel. (617) 253-5851
Lately, MIT's campus ha been attracting as many architecture buffs as it h rocket scientists. The $285 million Stata Cente designed by Frank Gehr and home to MIT's comp science and artificial intelligence lab, has no right angles and an irreg brick and metal façade.
MIT Museum (F F3)
→ 265 Massachusetts Ave
Tel. (617) 253-4444 Tue-Su
10am (noon Sat-Sun)–5pr
http://web.mit.edu/museu

SACKLER MUSEUM

FOGG ART MUSEUM

RADCLIFFE YARD

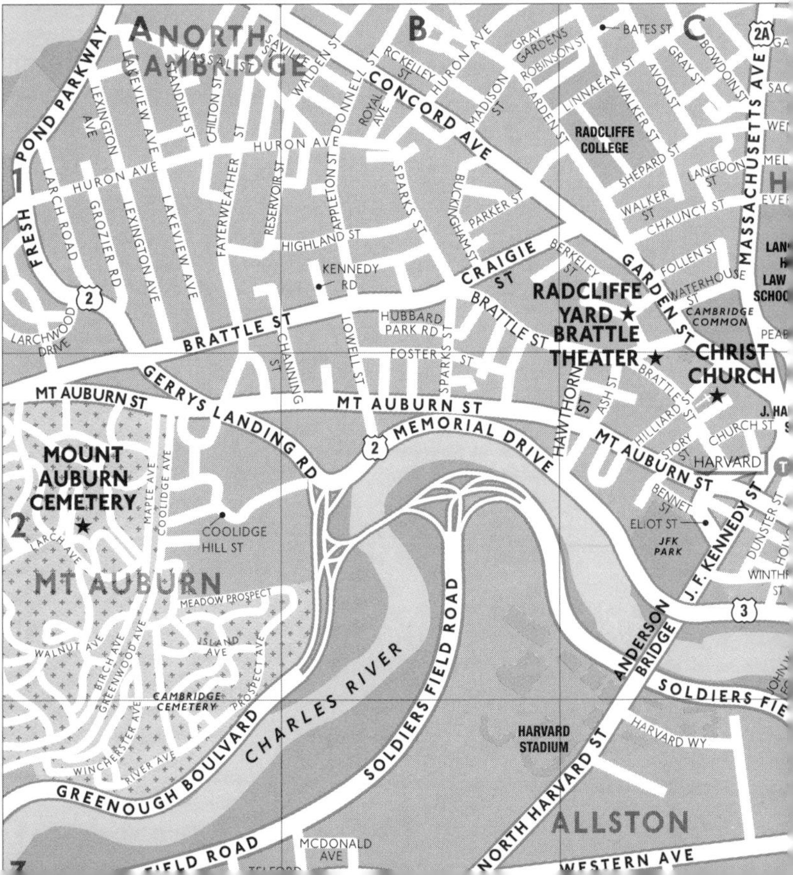

A
B
C
1
2
NORTH CAMBRIDGE
MT AUBURN
ALLSTON
MOUNT AUBURN CEMETERY
RADCLIFFE YARD
BRATTLE THEATER
CHRIST CHURCH
RADCLIFFE COLLEGE
HARVARD STADIUM
CAMBRIDGE CEMETERY
CAMBRIDGE COMMON
JFK PARK
HARVARD
CHARLES RIVER
POND PARKWAY
FRESH
LARCH ROAD
GROZIER RD
LEXINGTON AVE
LAKEVIEW AVE
STANDISH ST
CHILTON ST
FAYERWEATHER ST
RESERVOIR ST
APPLETON ST
DONNELL ST
WALDEN ST
SAVILLE ST
KASSAL ST
HURON AVE
CONCORD AVE
ROYAL AVE
SPARKS ST
BUCKINGHAM ST
PARKER ST
HIGHLAND ST
KENNEDY RD
CRAIGIE ST
BERKELEY ST
BRATTLE ST
HUBBARD PARK RD
FOSTER ST
LOWELL ST
CHANNING ST
LARCHWOOD DRIVE
MT AUBURN ST
GERRYS LANDING RD
MEMORIAL DRIVE
HAWTHORN ST
ASH ST
HILLIARD ST
STORY ST
CHURCH ST
BENNET ST
ELIOT ST
J. F. KENNEDY ST
DUNSTER ST
GARDEN ST
WATERHOUSE ST
FOLLEN ST
CHAUNCY ST
WALKER ST
SHEPARD ST
LANGDON ST
MASSACHUSETTS AVE
AVON ST
GRAY ST
BOWDOIN ST
LINNAEAN ST
GARDEN ST
ROBINSON ST
GRAY GARDENS
BATES ST
MADISON ST
KELLEY ST
COOLIDGE AVE
MAPLE AVE
COOLIDGE HILL ST
LARCH AVE
MEADOW PROSPECT
WALNUT AVE
BIRCH AVE
GREENWOOD AVE
ISLAND AVE
PROSPECT AVE
WINCHESTER AVE
RIVER AVE
GREENOUGH BOULVARD
SOLDIERS FIELD ROAD
ANDERSON BRIDGE
NORTH HARVARD ST
HARVARD WY
MCDONALD AVE
WESTERN AVE
2
2
3
2A

Cambridge

Across the Charles River, Cambridge is a sprawling collection of disparate neighborhoods. MIT and its surroundings have a geek chic feel, thanks to nearby Central Square and its abundance of live music venues and hipster bars. Just a short distance down Massachusetts Avenue, Harvard, the country's first college, remains an ivy-covered bastion of higher education. Harvard Square is an extension of the university and has an abundance of coffee shops, bookstores, good restaurants and bars. The outskirts of Harvard Square are lined with imposing mansions, and neighboring Inman and Davis squares are worth exploring for their local flavor and eclectic dining scenes.

UPSTAIRS ON THE SQUARE   RIALTO

RESTAURANTS

Bartley's (**F** D2)
→ 1246 Massachusetts Ave
Tel. (617) 354-6559
Mon-Sat 11am–9pm
This packed Harvard Square institution specializes in irreverently named burgers. Try the Ted Kennedy, a 'plump liberal burger with cheddar, mushrooms and French fries'. Almost as popular: the extra-thick frappes and the raspberry-lime rickeys. All burgers around $8.

Redbones BBQ (**F** off map north of B1)
→ 55 Chester St
Tel. (617) 628-2200 Daily 11am (noon Sun)–12.30am
This loud, colorful spot serves seriously good, bad-for-you Southern food: ribs, crispy fried catfish and juicy pulled pork. Beer connoisseurs head downstairs to Underbar for the specialty microbrews and late-night menu. À la carte $15.

Tamarind Bay (**F** C2)
→ 75 Winthrop St
Tel. (617) 491-4552 Daily 11.30am–2.30pm, 5–10pm
Descend into this cozy, bronze-toned space for the city's best Indian food. Sophisticated renditions of familiar tandoor dishes,
plus pleasant surprises: delicately spiced grilled scallops and rogan josh made with goat instead of lamb. Plenty of vegetarian options. À la carte $24.

East Coast Grill & Raw Bar (**F** E2)
→ 1271 Cambridge St
Tel. (617) 491-6568
Sun-Thu 5.30–10pm (10.30pm Fri-Sat); Sun 11am–2.30pm
Chef-owner Chris Schlesinger shows off his grilling mastery at this loud, lively Inman Square restaurant. Seafood entrees mix Latin America, Caribbean and Asian flavors, but the ribs are classic and delicious. For dessert, head a few doors down to Christina's Homemade Ice Cream. À la carte $30.

Dali (**F** E1)
→ 415 Washington St
Tel. (617) 661-3254
Daily 5.30pm–midnight
Costume jewelry as decor and strings of Christmas lights lend this tapas spot a playful atmosphere. On the menu are Spanish staples and exotic offerings such as roast duckling with berry sauce. Known for its long waits (no reservations), especially on Fri-Sat, but the potent sangria makes the time fly. À la carte $30.

EAST COAST GRILL AND RAW BAR

BLACK INK

Rialto (F C2)

→ *1 Bennet St, The Charles Hotel. Tel. (617) 661-5050 Mon-Sat 5.30–10pm (11pm Sat); Sun 5–9pm*
Celebrated chef Jody Adams turns out modern European cuisine at this elegant second-story restaurant. The ever-changing menu highlights fresh, locally sourced ingredients. À la carte $55.

Upstairs on the Square (F C2)

→ *91 Winthrop St Tel. (617) 864-1933 Monday Club Bar and Zebra Room: daily 11am–1am. Soiree Room: Tue-Sat 5.30–10pm (11pm Fri-Sat)*
Delicious New American fare is served in two equally fanciful dining rooms, the casual Monday Club Bar and Zebra Room, and, upstairs, the more formal Soiree Room. Menu includes kobe beef and striped bass upstairs and revamped classics downstairs. Popular brunch spot. À la carte $40 (Club Bar) and $60 (Soiree Room).

Oleana (F F2)

→ *134 Hampshire St Tel. (617) 661-0505 Daily 5.30–10pm (11pm Fri-Sat)*
In this pretty restaurant with a gardenlike outdoor patio, chef-owner Ana Sortun plays with traditional Mediterranean dishes and the results are astoundingly good; try the lamb with fava bean moussaka or the Armenian bean and walnut pate with homemade string cheese. The ice creams are legendary. À la carte $50.

BARS, CAFÉS, MUSIC VENUES

Darwin's Ltd Sandwich Shop (F C2)

→ *148 Mt Auburn St Tel. (617) 354-5233 Daily 7am–9pm (7pm Sun)*
This beloved coffeehouse/ gourmet food shop has unforgettable designer sandwiches, each named after a Cambridge street.

L.A. Burdick (F C2)

→ *52-D Brattle St Tel. (617) 491-4340 Daily 8am–9pm (10pm Thu-Sat)*
Famous for its rich hot chocolate – available in milk, dark, and white – this tiny jewelbox of a café prides itself on making all its beautiful confections by hand. Stake out one of the nine tables and have a hot drink and a slice of chocolate mousse cake.

Enormous Room (F E3)

→ *569 Massachusetts Ave Tel. (617) 491-5550 Daily 5.30pm–1am*
There's no sign for this painfully cool Moroccan lounge; just look for its parent restaurant, Central Kitchen, and head upstairs. Squeeze by the artfully disheveled hipsters and grab a spot on one of the low, pillow-strewn couches to enjoy the mix of funk, hip-hop, and reggae.

Herrell's Ice Cream (F C2)

→ *15 Dunster St Tel. (617) 497-2179 Daily 10am–midnight (1am Fri-Sat)*
An off-beat scoop shop in a former bank, whose specialty is spreading ice cream on a marble slab and 'smooshing in' the nuts, sprinkles, or fruits of choice.

SHOPPING

J. Press Clothiers (F C2)

→ *82 Mt Auburn St Tel. (617) 547-9886 Mon-Sat 9am–5pm*
From the days when Harvard was all-male, this civilized tailor still does a brisk business in bespoke shirts and suits, neckwear and a popular selection of bright ribbon belts.

The Tannery (F C2)

→ *11A Brattle St Tel. (617) 491-0810 Mon-Sat 9am–9pm (8pm Sat); Sun 10am–7pm*
Eclectic shop selling funky Kangaroo sneakers, all-weather boots, Lacoste separates and Northface fleeces. Known for predicting shoe trends.

Black Ink (F C2)

→ *5 Brattle St Tel. (617) 497-1221 Mon-Sat 10am–8pm; Sat 11am–7pm*
Floor-to-ceiling bookshelves packed with all manner of urban knick-knacks and fashionable home goods.

Harvard Book Store (F D2)

→ *1256 Massachusetts Ave Tel. (800) 542-7323 Mon-Sat 9am–11pm; Sun 10am–10pm*
This cozy two-floor shop has a wide selection of mainstream bestsellers, highbrow literature and, in the basement, remainders and used books. Popular author events.

Abodeon (F C1)

→ *1731 Massachussetts Ave Tel. (617) 497-0137 Mon-Sat 10am–6pm (8pm Thu & Sat); Sun noon–6pm*
Design aficionados come here for unique housewares and furnishings. This popular shop has a carefully edited collection of both vintage and modern items, from mint condition 1950s stoves to Hans Wegner sofas.

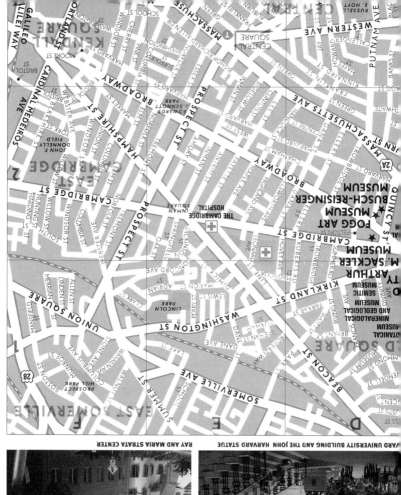

RAY AND MARIA STRATA CENTER

...YARD UNIVERSITY BUILDING AND THE JOHN HARVARD STATUE

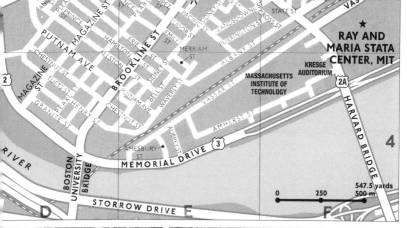

LE THEATER

MOUNT AUBURN CEMETERY

MIT Museum brings
her all that is high
and cutting edge.
main gallery showcases
world's largest
ography collection,
ding an eerily lifelike
e of the remains of the
o-year-old Lindlow
The satellite Hart
ical Gallery chronicles
istory of naval
tecture from clipper
to America's Cup
g yachts.

le Theater (F C2)
→ Brattle St
617) 876-6837
brattlefilm.org
rvard Square
ution since its live
ormance days in the

1900s. The single-screen
theater features everything
from Bugs Bunny to Hiroshi
Teshigahara, and book
readings cohosted by the
Harvard Book Store. The
theater is credited with
creating the country's first
'Bogie cults' when it began
a tradition of showing
Casablanca during Harvard
exam week.

Christ Church (F C2)
→ Zero Garden St
Tel. (617) 876-0200
Services Sun 8am, 10am;
Tue, Wed 12.10pm
Designed by Peter Harrison,
America's first architect,
this prim Georgian edifice
is Cambridge's oldest
church. Across from Harvard

Yard, it was founded in
1759 as an outpost of the
Church of England, and
now operates under the
Episcopalian denomination.
Radcliffe Yard (F C1)
Up Garden Street, this
remains a reminder of
Harvard College's formerly
separate sister school.
High school seniors know
this as the location of
the Harvard admissions
office, but cultural
historians are more
interested in the Arthur and
Elizabeth Schlesinger
Library, an important
collection of artifacts and
documents relating to
women's history. The
culinary collection of more

than 15,000 books includes
the personal papers of
celebrated food
connoisseurs M.F.K.
Fisher and Julia Child.
**Mount Auburn
Cemetery (F** A2)
→ 580 Mt Auburn St
Tel. (617) 547-7105 Daily
8am–5pm (7pm May-Sep)
With 175 bucolic acres of
rolling hills, placid ponds,
and thick woods, it is no
wonder that Boston's
elites – including Charles
Bulfinch, Isabella Stewart
Gardner, and Oliver
Wendell Holmes – chose
to be buried here. The
cemetery is known for its
horticulture, featuring more
than 700 varieties of flora.

Massachusetts Bay Transport Authority
www.mbta.com
For bus and subway info.

Subway
Inexpensive and quick, the 'T' can get you almost anywhere within the immediate city. Daily 5am–approx. 1am (depending on the stop). The new Silver Line links existing subway lines with high-tech hybrid buses that operate on normal roads as well as in underground tunnels via electric wires. The line will be fully completed by 2010.

Stations
Marked by large signs, they usually have designated 'Outbound' and 'Inbound' entrances. 'Inbound' will always be headed for the main hubs of Government Center, Park Street and Downtown Crossing.

Bus
About 170 routes. Maps are available at major T stations or online at *www.mbta.com.*

Fares
Tokens: $1.25 per ride for the T and the Silver Line; $0.90 per ride on buses. Tokens are available at subway stations; buses also accept exact change.

Visitors' passes
Unlimited travel on buses, subways and inner harbor ferries. One day: $7.50; three days: $18; seven days: $35.

Free travel
For children under 5.

ARNOLD ARBORETUM

JFK LIBRARY ATRIUM

DEPARTING FROM LONG WHARF FOR THE BOSTON ISLANDS

LITTLE BREWSTER ISLAND

$10 million upgrade a few years back, which included the addition of two trendy restaurants. Ask for a corner suite with working fireplace. $250–$350.

Hotel Marlowe (B A2)
→ 25 Edwin Land Blvd
Tel. (617) 868-8000
www.hotelmarlowe.com
Just across the Charles, this light-hearted hotel is close to MIT and just a short T ride from downtown. Tons of quirky extras: leopard print carpeting, complimentary kayaks and bikes, and special treatment for pets. $269–$330.

Boston Park Plaza Hotel & Towers (A F2)
→ 64 Arlington St
Tel. (617) 426-2000
www.bostonparkplaza.com
A self-proclaimed 'city within a city', this behemoth takes up a good part of the block,

with 941 elegant rooms and seven restaurants/ lounges. Theater-goers will appreciate the proximity to all the major shows. $275–$350.

Jurys Boston (A E2)
→ 350 Stuart St
Tel. (617) 266-7200
www.jurysdoyle.com
In 2004, the city's former police headquarters got a $60 million face-lift and was reborn as a 220-room hotel. An Irish sensibility prevails, from the warm service to the traditional pub. The Stanhope Grille serves hearty dinners and an Irish breakfast. $275–$395.

Marriott Custom House (C E1)
→ 3 McKinley Square
Tel. (617) 310-6300
www.marriott.com
This dramatic 1857 custom house was built to keep tabs on the harbor's comings and goings.

Easy access to the Financial District and waterfront activities make it popular with both the business crowd and families. $289–$329.

$300 and over

The Charles Hotel (west of F A4)
→ One Bennett St
Tel. (617) 864-1200
www.charleshotel.com
Dignitaries and politicians stay here during the Harvard portion of their lecture circuit. The rooms, with Shaker elements such as hand-made quilts and traditional furniture, strike a nice balance between modern and homey. You're guaranteed to eat well here: Henrietta's Table is a fresh-from-the-farm café with a popular Sunday brunch, and Rialto

AIRPORT

Logan International Airport
Tel. (800) 235-0426
www.massport.com/logan
New England's transportation hub. East of downtown, accessible via two major tunnels.
Getting downtown
By taxi
→ 20–30 mins ($15–$20);
By subway
→ 20 mins ($1.25).
By Silver Line
→ 15–20 mins ($1.25). This new line (see Public Transportation) is very helpful for getting between the airport and South Station.

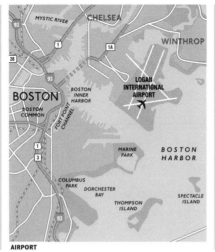

AIRPORT

TAXIS

While not as prevalent as in cities like New York, Boston cabs are useful for getting to out of the way places and late night transport. Call one of the companies listed below or hail them on the street.
Prices
$1.75 for the first 1/8 of a mile or less, then $0.30 for each additional 1/8 of a mile.
Service
15% of the fare charged
Taxi companies
Boston Cab
Tel. (617) 536-5010
Checker Cab
Tel. (617) 536-7000

Below is a listing of Boston's more notable lodgings.
• *While they skew toward the higher end, more budget-friendly accommodations are available at national chains such as Sheraton and Howard Johnson.*
• *Except where otherwise stated, prices given are for a double room with bath during high season (June–Aug, Sep–Oct). Hotel tax (12.45%) is not included.*
• *Advance reservations are highly recommended.*

$160–$200

Midtown Hotel (A B4)
220 Huntington Ave
Tel. (617) 262-1000
www.midtownhotel.com
A 1960s-style motor court lodge well located near the Prudential Center. Slightly dingy decor

notwithstanding, the rooms are large and clean. Complimentary parking makes this a great budget option. $130–$190.
Hotel 140 (A D2)
→ 140 Clarendon St
Tel. (617) 585-5600
www.hotel140.com
This new hotel is a first for Back Bay: affordable rooms that won't make you cringe. With views of the Hancock Tower outside your window, free wireless and cable TV, you'll hardly feel like you're on a budget. $160–$186.
The Charlesmark Hotel (A C2)
→ 655 Boylston St
Tel. (617) 247-1212
www.thecharlesmark.com
Urban chic digs on discount: this boutique hotel across from Copley Square is surprisingly reasonable. The 33 rooms feature clean,

contemporary lines and fun accents: offbeat wall art and fresh flowers. Continental breakfast. $169–$199.

$200–$300

Fairmont Copley Plaza (A D2)
→ 138 St James Ave
Tel. (617) 267-5300
www.fairmont.com
This hotel's scarlet awnings and regal façade have bordered Copley Square since 1912, but a recent upgrade has freshened the 383 suites. Lots of dark woods and marble. $229–$379.
Omni Parker House (B D5)
→ 60 School St
Tel. (617) 227-8600
www.omnihotels.com
Perfect for history buffs, the country's oldest continuously operating hotel has hosted everyone

from Charles Dickens to John F. Kennedy. It has a great location off the Freedom Trail. $235–$305.
Beacon Hill Hotel (B B5)
→ 25 Charles St
Tel. (617) 723-7575
www.beaconhillhotel.com
With 12 smartly decorated rooms and a private roof deck, this boutique hotel could easily be mistaken for just another Brahmin mansion. The gourmet eateries and upscale shops of Charles Street are steps away, and the in-house bistro is popular with well-heeled 20-somethings. $245–$305.
Lenox Hotel (A C2)
→ 61 Exeter St
Tel. (617) 536-5300
www.lenoxhotel.com
A grand family-owned hotel near the Public Library. The turn-of-the-century building got a

Transportation in Boston

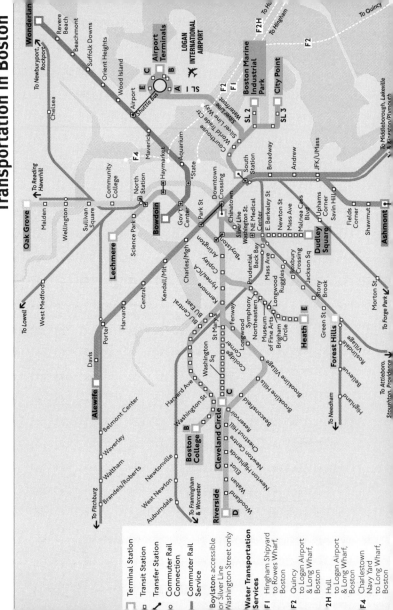

Legend

- ☐ Terminal Station
- ☐ Transit Station
- ☐ Transfer Station
- ✕ Commuter Rail Connection
- ○ Commuter Rail Service

Boylston: accessible or Silver Line Washington Street only

Water Transportation Services

F1 Hingham Shipyard to Rowes Wharf, Boston

F2 Quincy to Logan Airport & Long Wharf, Boston

2H Hull to Logan Airport & Long Wharf, Boston

F4 Charlestown Navy Yard to Long Wharf, Boston

Street names, monuments and places to visit are listed alphabetically. They are followed by a map reference, of which the initial letter(s) in bold (**A, B, C**...) relate to the matching map(s) within this guide.

Boston Harbor Islands
→ *Harbor Express has daily ferries leaving from Long Wharf near Columbus Park Tel. (617) 223-8666 www.bostonislands.com www.harborexpress.com/ harborislands/*
Pack a picnic lunch and hop on a ferry for a pleasant day trip. These 34 picturesque islands range from 1 to 274 acres in size. Only the 11 islands open to the public are shown on the map (right). They include Georges Island, home of Fort Warren. Free water taxis let you hop between islands.

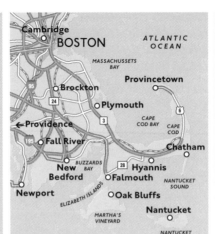

EXCURSIONS

Cape Cod
→ *The Sagamore Bridge, which links the Cape to the mainland, is 30 miles from Boston. During high season traffic can get backed up for hours. Daily ferries from Boston to Provincetown. www.capecodchamber.org*
Beginning with Falmouth, just 1 ½ hrs from Boston, elbow-shaped Cape Cod has more than 70 miles of remarkably uncluttered beachfront along the Atlantic Ocean and Nantucket Sound. The downside to all this beauty is that during the summer it seems as if all of New England is there. Provincetown, best accessed by a one-hour fast ferry from Boston, is known for its vibrant gay community and fun atmosphere.

Martha's Vineyard
→ *7 miles off Cape Cod. www.mvy.com. Accessible from Boston via ferry from Cape Cod (45 mins) or via air (30 mins, www.flycapeair.com).*
The summertime destination of literary, political and showbiz celebrities, including the Clintons, this charming island is a beautiful escape.

Nantucket
→ *26 miles off Cape Cod. Accessible via short flight or ferry from Hyannis or Woods Hole. www.nantucket.net*
A former whaling town turned beach playground for the wealthy, Nantucket still charms with its winding streets and gorgeous beaches.

your luxury. The Ritz-Carlton Boston is a 1927 landmark that still maintains elements of Gilded Age extravagance – its location on Newbury makes it easy to pop into Burberry for a quick outfit change before drinks overlooking the Public Garden. Across the park, the younger and hipper Ritz-Carlton Boston Common has a $1 million modern art collection and a partnership with the see-and-be-seen Sports Club LA. Rates are slightly lower. $350–$579.

XV Beacon (B C-D5)
→ *15 Beacon St Tel. (617) 670-1500 www.xvbeacon.com*
This 61-room boutique hotel specializes in tasteful indulgence. Thoughtful details include working fireplaces, heated towel bars and the ultimate luxury – a fleet of Lexus sedans at your disposal. Non-guests come to The Federalist for celebrated reimagined American cuisine. $350–$500.

Nine Zero Hotel (B D5)
→ *90 Tremont St Tel. (617) 772-5800 www.ninezero.com*
Design-minded travelers will appreciate the sophisticated Modernist style – striped bedspreads in neutral tones and furniture in unusual silhouettes – of this boutique hotel. And if you decide you just can't live without that art-deco side table, just reach for your AmEx – almost everything in the room is for sale. $379–$459.

Four Seasons (A F1)
→ *200 Boylston St Tel. (617) 338-4400 www.fourseasons.com*
Impeccable service and peerless views of the Public Garden make this a top pick among high-end travelers. The 273 rooms feature 19th-century Beacon Hill decorative elements and 21st-century technological amenities. The main restaurant, Aujourd'hui, serves world-class French nouvelle cuisine in a very ornate setting. $395–$550.

Boston Harbor Hotel (C F2)
→ *70 Rowes Wharf Tel. (617) 439-7000 www.bhh.com*
You can take a water taxi directly from the airport to this deluxe 230-room property. During the summer, locals gather on the hotel's pavilion for free movie screenings and concerts. Meritage is known for serving impressive food and wine – with a priceless view of the harbor. $405–$480.

South Boston
John Fitzgerald Kennedy Library & Museum
→ *Columbia Point, at Morrissey Blvd Columbia Point; take the red line to JFK/UMASS station. Shuttle buses labeled JFK circulate every 20 mins. Tel. (617) 514-1600 Daily 9am–5pm www.jfklibrary.org*
This tribute to the 35th president, designed by I. M. Pei, is set on a 10-acre park overlooking Dorchester Bay. Among the artifacts: handwritten notes, archival photographs and recorded conversations. The permanent exhibit on First Lady Jacqueline Bouvier Kennedy is especially popular.

Arnold Arboretum
→ *Jamaica Plain, 125 The Arborway (20–30 minutes from central Boston on the T. Take the orange line to Forest Hills stop). Tel. (617) 524-1718 www.arboretum.harvard.edu Daily sunrise–sunset. Tours available Sat, Sun and Wed.*
The most impressive member of the Emerald Necklace, this 265-acre park is a maze of paths, hills, ponds and gardens. Pick up a map at the Hunnewall Visitors center and see how many of the over 4,500 varieties of greenlife you can spot; there is everything from honey locust trees to horse chestnuts. In mid-May, the garden holds Lilac Sunday, a daylong celebration with dancing, tours and picnicking.

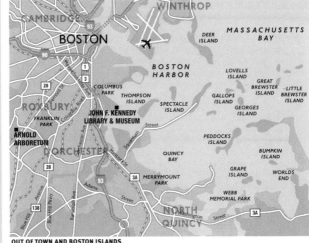

OUT OF TOWN AND BOSTON ISLANDS

is among of the city's finest. $279–$500.
Langham Hotel (C D1-2)
→ *250 Franklin St Tel. (617) 451-1900 www.langhamhotels.com/langham/boston*
Convenient to the Financial District, this favorite of businesspeople is appropriately set in the former Federal Reserve. All 325 suites feature lavish neo-Renaissance decor. Dining is no less impressive: Julien is one of the city's most extravagant French restaurants. $300–$375.
Eliot Hotel (E F1)
→ *370 Commonwealth Ave Tel. (617) 267-1607 www.eliothotel.com*
On the edge of Back Bay, this intimate hotel prides itself on attracting a hyper-discerning clientele. The slightly out-of-the-way location is

more than made up for by the fact that 24-hour room service is available from Clio, the city's hottest Japanese fusion spot and a James Beard Award winner. $300–$450.
Onyx Hotel (B D3)
→ *155 Portland St Tel. (617) 557-0005 www.onyxhotel.com*
Near the TD Banknorth Garden, this boutique property has an optic motif with cherry-red accents. Perks include a nightly wine hour and free morning town car service to business meetings. Tweens love the Britney Spears Foundation room, designed to mirror the pop princess's girlhood room (10% of the room rate goes to charity). $320–$375.
Hotel Commonwealth (E E1)
→ *500 Commonwealth Ave Tel. (617) 933-5000*

www.hotelcommonwealth.com
A posh sleep option right around the corner from Fenway Park. While Red Sox fans will just be happy to be close to the motherland, everyone else will appreciate the warm modern decor, L'Occitane bath goodies and fantastic Great Bay (see **E**), the sister restaurant of Radius (see **C**). $329–$389.

LUXURY HOTELS

Ritz-Carlton Boston (A E1)
→ *15 Arlington St Tel. (617) 536-5700 www.ritzcarlton.com*
Ritz-Carlton Boston Common (C B3)
→ *10 Avery St Tel. (617) 574-7100 www.ritzcarlton.com*
These two hotels give you a choice of how you want